YOUTH TACKLE FOOTBALL

A Guide to Teaching Safer Football and Preventing Injuries

Alan Jackson

ISBN: 978-0692457788

Published by:
Castle Rock Press, LLC
12379 S. 265 West, Suite F
Draper, Utah 84020

Youth Tackle Football/Alan Jackson
First edition

Contributing Photographer: Dave Sanderson

Editor and Content Designer: Mary Jo Stresky, The Write MoJo Literary and Research Services: www.thewritemojo.com

DISCLAIMER:

Neither the author nor the publisher shall be held liable or responsible to any person or entity with respect to any injury or incidental or consequential damages caused, or alleged to have been caused, directly or indirectly, by the information or strategies contained herein, as the advice and strategies contained herein may not be suitable for your own unique situation.

The author claims no ability or expertise to determine the cause or diagnosis of any injury, and therefore won't be discussing the validity of such claims in this book.

The rigors of football can be dangerous if not practiced safely. If you're in doubt as to how to proceed or whether the practice is safe for your children or the youth you're working with, please consult with a trained athletic instructor before beginning. Since the physical activities described herein may be too strenuous in nature for some youth, it's also essential that a physician be consulted prior to training.

Best efforts have been used in preparing this material which is presented solely within this book for educational and informative purposes. The author and publisher make no representations or warranties of any kind, and assume no liabilities of any kind with respect to the accuracy or completeness of the contents.

While all attempts have been made to verify all information provided within this publication, the publisher and author assume no responsibility for errors, omissions, or contrary interpretations of the subject matter herein. Any perceived slights of specific persons, peoples, or organizations are unintentional.

TABLE OF CONTENTS

INTRODUCTION

My name is Alan Jackson. And no, I'm not the rich, handsome Country Western singer (I get asked that all the time).

I grew up in Murray, Utah, where football wasn't very prominent. The sports available to kids were baseball and motocross, and the only thing I remember about football was our high school team wasn't very good (sorry, guys – it's true).

Two of my sons have played football, my third is thinking of playing youth tackle football, and my two daughters have played very well in basketball. Therefore, my family has experienced its share of injuries including a broken collarbone and dislocated ribs (my sons), which was part of the impetus for writing this book.

I've been coaching youth tackle football on and off for many years, and this will be my fourth season at Riverton High. In addition to football, I've also coached basketball and baseball at the youth Super League level.

Coaching is a great passion of mine and I take it very seriously. I'll be comprehensively discussing tackle football at the youth level, the coaches who manage the sport, the upsides and pitfalls of today's equipment, and what parents can do to help prevent injuries to their children.

Playing Hurt Versus Playing Injured

A tendency among some coaches is to say, "Play hurt, but not injured." The obvious flaw in that statement is their inability or lack of education to be able to determine if the player is hurt versus seriously injured.

"The [best] coaches... know that the job is to win... know that they must be decisive, that they must phase people through their organizations, and at the same time they are sensitive to the feelings, loyalties, and emotions that people have toward one another. If you don't have these feelings, I do not know how you can lead anyone. I have spent many sleepless nights trying to figure out how I was going to phase out certain players for whom I had strong feelings, but that was my job. I wasn't hired to do anything but win."

~Bill Walsh, Head Coach of the San Francisco 49ers and the Stanford Cardinal football team, and sports broadcaster

There are situations when you know just by looking at a player that they're obviously injured. But most of the time there are no visible, conclusive signs that something is wrong.

A few years ago our high school team was playing against our rival school, and on a kick return our player returning the ball was tackled in a way that broke his arm. It was obvious he was injured since his forearm was pointing in the wrong direction (not a good sign!). That same season another player had three dislocated ribs – a non-evident injury invisible to the eye. The doctor confirmed that playing wouldn't cause any further harm, and cleared him to play the remainder of the season in spite of being injured.

Imagine a coach asking a 9, 10 or 11-year-old, "Are you injured, or just hurt?" Because they don't know any better, the young player answers, "I'm just hurt," to which the coach says, "Well, get back in the game!" The kid returns to the game with an injury that could become worse the longer he plays, and have long-term consequences.

A dirty little secret is if the player is a star player, a coach will often send him back into the game. But if he's a player of lesser talent, they're sent to the bench to recover.

The decision to hold or play is therefore in the hands of someone who makes a selfish decision for the team (and often themselves) as opposed to a well-informed diagnosis to protect the player.

The glaring question then is does that young player (no matter their age) and/or the coach have the expertise to determine if the player is hurt or injured? If not, should regulations about education be in place to make sure the coach can make the best decisions for their team?

As a coach and a parent of a player in Little League football, I've witnessed coaches who have encouraged and even forced players to play with an injury. So I'll be discussing the following underlying questions throughout the book: Is there danger in youth tackle football itself? Or in the coaches and leagues that manage the sport? Or both?

While discussing these issues I'll be using experiences, examples and quotes from football and other sports to illustrate the influence coaches have on their players.

Coaching is a privilege that far too many people take for granted. The influence a coach can have on their players is substantial and enduring, and therefore must be held in the highest regard.

Questioning the Safety of Tackle Football

If you find yourself questioning the safety of youth tackle football, what event caused you ask questions? For me, and I'm sure for many of you, it's the media coverage related to the long-term effects of playing football.

Personally, I question anything coming out of today's news as it's often skewed for entertainment purposes. So I prefer to make decisions based on my own research (which is correct to do as a coach).

In no way would I ever suggest the tragedies families and loved ones have experienced due to football injuries isn't real or devastating. Even though two of my sons experienced injuries while playing football I never questioned the safety of the sport, but rather attributed the injuries to bad luck.

That is, until I researched content for this book which changed my views on the safety of youth tackle football.

There have been tragedies with high school, college and professional players that have caused people to question the safety of football in general. However, much of the conflict is related to issues of mental illness or memory loss that's often attributed to the many head impacts and concussions players receive during practice and games.

All in the Name of Winning

The drive to win can be a powerful force. So powerful in fact that at times it causes administrators, coaches and players to cheat.
If you've ever seen the movie *Cool Runnings* with John Candy, you'll remember that while competing at the sport of Bobsled in the Olympics, his character, Irv, placed weights in his bobsled to make it go faster. He cheated and was caught and banned for life from competing as an athlete.

Disgraced and without friends, he moved to Jamaica where, through a series of fortuitous events, he becomes the coach of the Jamaican bobsled team that qualified for the Olympics. When one of his teammates asks him why he cheated he answered, "I had to win." Obviously this is just a movie, but it resonates far too often with real life.

Adhering to Boundaries

In *Cool Runnings*, in addition to telling the team "I had to win," Irv says something I find very profound with regard to winning the gold medal: "If you're not enough without it, you will never be enough with it." Although it isn't supposed to be allowed, there are high school programs that recruit players from outside their boundaries. Since everyone knows it happens, it can be assumed the governing body over high school sports knows about it and yet does nothing to prevent it.

A coach with a powerful and well-trained booster club never needs to encourage or ask them to recruit for him. So is there a difference if a school's booster club members are recruiting on behalf of the coach, or if the coach himself is recruiting? Maybe. But there really shouldn't be.

For example, in some areas of Utah youth pre-high school football players aren't allowed to play for a team outside their high school boundaries. If caught, they're banned from playing the rest of the season, and the team's wins with them on the field are stricken from the record.

Once these teens attend the first day of high school and try out for a team, they're forced to play within their high school boundaries. Utah has open enrollment for sports, so prior to attending the first day of high school or trying out for a team a student may choose to attend a different school. However, once they're bound to their home school, they can only transfer and play sports with permission of the Utah High School Activities Association.

Imagine your son playing youth football with your high school's name on his jersey all the way up to high school, then attends tryouts to make the high school team.

Having been around the youth football program for several years, you'd more than likely recognize most of the players coming up from the youth program. But when you pick him up from tryouts, you don't recognize many of the kids.

At the end of tryouts your son (who's dedicated his entire football career to that particular high school) is cut from the team. You learn that many players who made the team came in from outside the high school boundary ... all in the name of *winning*.

Driving Competition

In sports the competition and drive to be the best continually increases an athlete's abilities. According to Wikipedia, in 1900 the record for the men's 100 meters (held by many including Americans Frank Harris and Walter Tewksbury) was 10.8 minutes. It wasn't until 1968 when Americans Jim Hynes, Ronnie Ray Smith, and Charles Green broke the 10.0 mark with a 9.9 time.

In 2009, Usain Bolt recorded a time of 9.58 minutes. More than 100 years had passed between the 10.8 recorded time and when Bolt shaved more than a full second off the event.

Since it had been the contention of experts for many years that the human body wasn't capable of running a four-minute mile, it was widely accepted that it would be impossible to achieve.

However, according to the IAAF (International Association of Athletics Federation) the record for running the four-minute mile was held by American John Paul Jones at 4:14.4 in 1913. In 1945, the Swedish runner, Gunder Hägg set the record at 4:01.4, which would stand as the record for nine years.

In 1954 Roger Bannister from the United Kingdom broke Hägg's record, and successfully accomplished what experts had said couldn't be done. On May 6, 1954, while running at Oxford, Bannister broke the four-minute mile threshold with a record time of 3:59.04.

You can look at athletes throughout history who were so driven by competition that they took the sport to a higher level by exceeding what anyone had previously accomplished. Certain players who immediately come to mind are...

- Basketball: Oscar Robertson, Michael Jordan, Larry Bird and Magic Johnson
- Boxing: Muhammad Ali, Mike Tyson, Sugar Ray Leonard and Joe Frazier
- Baseball: Babe Ruth, Hank Aaron, Lou Gehrig, Cal Ripken, Jr., and Willie Mays

Just when you think a sport can't get any better, faster, or stronger, someone arrives on the scene and takes it to the next level with their need to be the best of the best.

Is an athlete's drive to be the best drive the impetus behind the invention of the equipment they use? Or does the invention of the equipment drive the athletes to the next level?

I'd suggest that chicken-and-egg question is true on both sides. As sports progress, and the ceiling is raised to the next level, innovations to the equipment specific to that sport must keep up-to-date.

There are times when the innovation of the equipment allows for an athlete's performance to increase. I've witnessed a basketball player with great talent and ability playing with worn out sneakers, and wondered how much better their performance could have been if they were wearing a new pair of basketball shoes.

Things to Consider

When considering the safety of tackle football, we must be mindful of the different aspects that effect the players' well-being as it is no different when it comes to the game's ever-increasing level of competition.

Conditioning and proper stretching can minimize injuries, including concussions from excessive head impact. Proper tackling and impact techniques can't be over-emphasized for keeping players safe. And of course, quality equipment plays a vital role in player safety.

Therefore, it's my goal to provide you with the proper information to make a well-informed, educated decision about the current **safety standards of youth tackle football**.

CHAPTER ONE

HISTORY OF THE FOOTBALL HELMET

"When I played pro football, I never set out to hurt anyone deliberately - unless it was, you know, important, like a league game or something."
~Dick Butkus, Chicago Bears Linebacker

Organized football began around 1860, but it wasn't until 1893 that a helmet of any kind was worn while playing the game. Prior to then, players played bareheaded and took their chances against incurring life-threatening injuries.

Early 1900s
Soft leather harness style.
YMCA team from Latrobe, Pennsylvania.
1915
Soft leather flat-top style.
Typical of early pro team Canton Bulldogs.
YMCA team from Latrobe, Pennsylvania.
1920s
Soft leather helmet.
Typical of the NFL's Duluth Eskimos.
1930s, early 1940s
Hard leather style.
Typical of the NFL's Chicago Bears.
1940s
Hard leather,
first graphics.
Los Angeles Rams.
1950s, 1960s
Plastic helmet.
Detroit Lions.
1970s, early 1980s
Plastic helmet.
St. Louis Cardinals.
1980s to present
Plastic helmet,
Minnesota Vikings.
Riddell Revolution helmet.
ProCap, a polyurethane pad that attaches to the outside of the helmet, is an added safeguard against concussions.

When his doctor warned him that another blow to his head could cause permanent brain damage, Joseph Mason Reeves (a midshipman at the Naval Academy) had an Annapolis cobbler construct a leather helmet to protect his skull. Reeves wore this history-making helmet during the Army-Navy game:

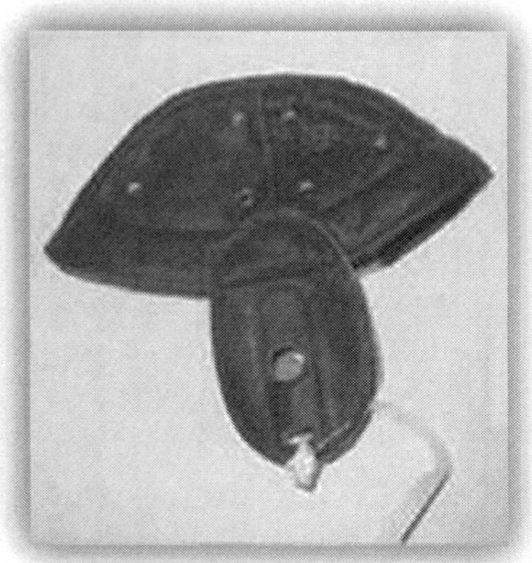

In 1896, George Barclay (Lafayette University) crafted a head harness out of three straps of hard leather that was supposed to prevent a "cauliflower ear":

As you can see below, Knute Rockne (football player and coach for Notre Dame) wasn't wearing any of the padding currently found in football gear. If you think about the physicality of today's football game relying on this lack of equipment for protection, you can imagine the amount of injuries that occurred before football became safer.

Knute Rockne 1906

Though helmets arrived on the scene in 1893 (more "hats" really, as they didn't offer much protection), they weren't required to be worn by the National Football League (NFL).

The leather helmet was worn by a few players until the first plastic helmet was produced by John Riddell in 1939. Until then, for 46 years the leather helmet was the safest innovation the sport had to offer. In 1940, Dick Plasman of the Chicago Bears was the last professional football player to play without a helmet. The fact that it took that long for wearing a helmet to become mandatory by the NFL reaffirms the safety factor in any sport is greatly influenced by the need for equipment, coaches and League officials.

Fortunately, the NFL is much more conscientious and aggressive today about governing the protection of its players (although it still needs improvement).

"Crazy Legs" Elroy Hirsch - 1948 Rams

You'll notice that Hirsch's helmet doesn't have a face mask. The single bar face mask, like some kickers wear today, wasn't introduced until 1955. But it took seven more years until it was added to all helmets being used in the NFL.

Evolution of the football helmet took its next step when the air bladder was introduced in 1971 to help lessen the impact.

Today's Helmets

There have been many innovative advances with the helmet over the years, along with other gear such as the increased effectiveness of shoulder pads. It's hard to imagine that until the NFL required every player to wear a helmet, players were playing bareheaded.

As is usually the case in the entrepreneurial world, innovations increase the more competition becomes involved. Just as the athlete is driven to be the best and better than their competition, driven entrepreneurs push new technology and inventions through the roof.

This was the case with regard to the helmet and other football equipment. With the entries into the marketplace such as Xenith's X2, Rawlings Quantum Plus, and Schutt's Ion 4D, the protection offered by helmets has been greatly improved. Advancement in design has gone even a step further with Bill Simpson's creation of the SGH Helmet that uses carbon fiber and a Kevlar shell.

It's easy to see how the focus on safety in football, as well as the increased skill level and the speed of the game, have produced equipment like the above helmets to help prevent injuries. Even though injuries can still occur, advancement in technology has done a great deal to lessen and even prevent injuries that otherwise would have occurred.

I shudder to think of football players playing in today's games without helmets and virtually no other padding. The resulting injuries would be devastating for both the players and the American Football League.

CHAPTER TWO

THE SAFETY OF YOUTH FOOTBALL CALLED INTO QUESTION

"Football is not a contact sport-it is a collision sport. Dancing is a contact sport."
~Duffy Daugherty, Michigan State

In an interview with Tom Farrey titled *Study: Impact of Youth Head Hits Severe* (video and article available on ESPN; URL link in References), Lisa McHale – the wife of former NFL player, Tom McHale -- shared how their life was impacted by the game of football.

The report reveals that after leaving football, and while dealing with chronic pain, Tom became addicted to prescription drugs which later led to the use of other drugs. After he passed away in May of 2008 from an accidental overdose, the autopsy revealed he was suffering from a progressive degenerative brain disease known as Chronic Traumatic Encephalopathy or (CTE).

Apparently CTE can't be proven to be directly related to the game of football, although the disease is a direct result of too many impacts to the head and body.

Since the general public doesn't typically experience those types of traumatic impacts, a conclusion can be drawn that Tom's injuries weren't a direct result of playing football and receiving way too many impacts to his brain.

During the interview, Lisa shared her feelings regarding the game of football and why her sons aren't allowed to play: "You have to understand that I lost my very best friend, and my kids lost their dad. Sometimes it just amazes me that my kids are fatherless, and that just seems like way too heavy a price to pay to play a game."

Headline: "America's Most Dangerous Football is in the Pee-Wee Leagues, Not the NFL"

In his story written in August of 2013 (URL in References), Allen Barra examines the documentary by Sean Pamphilon called "The United States of Football." (Pamphilon has been awarded an Emmy as well as a Peabody for his filmmaking; you can visit his website via the URL in References to watch his video, and information about his work.)

His heart-wrenching, frightening documentary discusses the damage to the brain from playing football. At the beginning of the video you'll hear him say... "The road to this journey began with the decision to let my own 12-year-old son play, the acronym CTE, and the story I read about Kyle Turley: [Turley] 'It can lead to other really bad things, you know. Onsets of dementia, Alzheimer's Disease. Not really looking forward to that'."

NOTE: Kyle John Turley (born September 24, 1975) is a former American college and professional football player who was an offensive tackle in the National Football League (NFL) for ten seasons. He played college football at San Diego State, and was recognized as an All-American.

He was originally drafted by the New Orleans Saints seventh overall in the 1998 NFL Draft, and played professionally for the Saints, St. Louis Rams and Kansas City Chiefs of the NFL. He was an All-Pro selection in 2000. Turley currently works as a country music recording artist, and is a prominent voice in debate over the effects of concussions the post-career health of NFL players.

Chief neuropathologist at Boston University, Dr. Ann McKee, has testified before the United States House of Representatives Judiciary Committee regarding brain injuries in football. In Pamphilon's documentary she explains that "because a young athlete's brain is still developing, the effects of a concussion, or even many smaller hits over a season, can be far more detrimental, compared to the head injury in an older player."

The film also includes comments from Chris Carter, a former NFL great, in which he states, "Our best coaches are coaching our best players, and that's in professional football. Our worst coaches are coaching the most critical position, and that is the 9, 10, 11 year-old people." Pamphilon adds, "At this level, you have no idea what a coach's qualifications are as an instructor or his maturity as a man."

According to USA Football (the national governing body in Indiana for amateur American football), there are more than three million players in the youth football programs across the country ranging in ages from 6 to 14.

In my experience there are typically around 20 players per team, which would require around 150,000 head coaches to manage that many players. At four coaches per team, it would require around 600,000 coaches to coach all the youth football programs in across America.

One of the greatest challenges to safety in youth football is the lack of adequate and informed coaching that's being discussed in length on many websites and blogs. I personally experienced this years ago where I was allowed to coach, having never previously played or coached football.

Today, in the youth program I was involved in coaches are required to go through a training of about three to four hours every three years in order to maintain certification. Over the last few years our local league has expanded the training to include proper pre-contact stretching, which is required prior to any padded practice or game.

No Tackle Football Until Age 14

In a book written by Mark Hyman, *Concussions and Our Kids: America's Leading Expert on How to Protect Young Athletes and Keep Sports Safe* (which he co-authored with Dr. Robert Cantu, a clinical professor of neurosurgery at the Boston University School of Medicine), a good argument is made that tackle football should not be allowed until age 14.

In an article for TIME.com, Mark Hyman makes the following arguments for establishing the age limit at 14 years old):

> "Kids are not miniature adults. By age 4, the heads of kids are 90% of adult size. However, their necks are much weaker than an adult's neck. The combination creates a danger. When a child takes a hard blow from falling or being struck in the helmet, it is more difficult to keep the head steady. The result is greater force to the brain from being jerked inside the skull.
>
> Kids don't understand the risks. This is as much an ethical as a medical consideration. A teenager entering high school can make a judgment about the ups and downs of playing tackle football. He has the ability to think through the consequences himself, not as an adult would but at least with an understanding of risk and reward. The same isn't true of a 6-year-old.
>
> Much is not known about the long-term effects of repetitive head trauma, especially among young children. How will these kids be affected when they're 70, or even 50?"

Hyman recommends flag football should be played until age 14. There's no tackling, and the players wear flags that hang down from each side of their waist. As soon as a flag is removed from a player by a member of the opposite team, the ball is dead at that spot.

This would allow the young players to learn all aspects of the sport of football – including tackling they practice on dummies – and not have to endure the hardship of being physical tackled and injured.

The case has been made by many others that the minimum age for beginning tackle football should be set by leagues or by parents themselves. Tom Brady, Sr. -- the father of future Hall of Fame quarterback for the New England Patriots, Tom Brady, Jr., -- didn't allow his son to play tackle football until he was a freshman in high school. Concerned about injuries that might include concussions, as a parent he made the decision to not allow Tom to play until he was 14.

Legendary BYU Football coach, Lavell Edwards, has also stated he wouldn't recommend beginning tackle football until they reach the high school level.

Having watched my sons go through many injuries – including a concussion -- I've determined that the better informed and educated parents and coaches are about the pitfalls of tackle football, the less likely players will sustain injuries.

CHAPTER THREE

THE COACHES

"Winning records are an extremely limiting and inaccurate way to judge the quality and effectiveness of a coach. Simply put, winning doesn't make you a good coach in the same way that losing doesn't make you a bad one. The fact of the matter is that judging a coach's abilities and effectiveness based on the record of his/her team is to totally miss the complexity behind good and bad coaching."
~Dr. Alan Goldberg

NOTE: *Even though this book is on tackle football, as I previously stated I'm also going to share some of my observations about how coaches in other sports, such as basketball, have great influence over their players.*

It's astounding how much long-term influence a coach can have on young players. The opportunity to have a tremendous impact and be solid role models is what makes coaching an amazing experience.

Sadly, far too many coaches miss these opportunities due to their lack of sportsmanship and respect for the game, and focusing just on winning.

"Coach" is a title that's not to be taken lightly, as the positive influence of being a coach can reach far beyond the game itself. They're held in such high esteem that movies have been made about them, including...

- *The Bear* (1984 – Alabama's Bear Bryant – football)
- *Remember the Titans* (2000 – Herman Boone – football)
- *Miracle* (2004 – re. Herb Brooks – hockey)

Many movies have also been produced that included great coaching motivational speeches such as the following from coach Brooks (Kurt Russell) in *Miracle on Ice* (URLs and quotes can be found in section on Motivational Quotes):

> "Great moments are born from great opportunity, and that's what you have here tonight, boys. That's what you've earned here tonight. One game; if we played them ten times, they might win nine. But not this game, not tonight. Tonight, we skate with them.
>
> Tonight we stay with them, and we shut them down because we can. Tonight, we are the greatest hockey team in the world. You were born to be hockey players -- every one of you - and you were meant to be here tonight. This is your time. Their time is done. It's over.
>
> I'm sick and tired of hearing about what a great hockey team the Soviets have. Screw 'em. This is your time. Now go out there and take it!"

The mindset of a player going into a game can set them up for a win or a fall, and the support, nurturing and approval from the coach means everything. Coaches who put the team before the win can be guaranteed a "win" even if the team loses.

"What Makes A Good Coach?"

I read an article by Dr. Alan Goldberg (URL in Motivational Quotes at end of book; all 20 characteristics listed below) who wrote about the twenty characteristics of a good coach following a conversation he had with a freshman baseball player playing at a Division One college.

Although only a freshman, this young athlete playing on a full ride scholarship had earned a starting position on the baseball team. He was playing at a competitive level in the field as well as at the plate, which allowed him to beat older and more experienced teammates for the starting position of second baseman.

He'd come through for his team in very important games including one where he batted three for four against a rival team driving in two runs.

Performing at what most would consider a high level, especially for a freshman, this player through a series of comments, threats and humiliation by his coaches was absolutely destroyed as a player and devastated as a person:

> "A few weeks before the beginning of the conference tournament he was at the peak of his game. He went 3 for 4 in a critical match-up with the team's perennial rival, driving in two runs with two singles and a double. After the game his head coach pulled him aside and congratulated him on a great game and for how well he had been playing.
>
> Then, in the same breath, the coach told his freshman that he needed him hitting more home runs. The skipper explained that he had recruited him because of his bat and that the team's success heavily depended upon him hitting more of the long balls.
>
> At first this player was totally confused by the coach's comments and even thought that perhaps the man might just be pulling his leg. However, when he realized that the coach was actually dead serious, his confusion turned to dismay and then anger." ~Dr. Alan Goldberg

The outcome of such a comment is predictable by most, if not all, good coaches. Telling a baseball player to "swing for the fence!" is never a good idea, and can only lead to a diminishing performance.

Unfortunately, that's exactly what happened to the athlete mentioned above. For the first time since he began playing baseball, he questioned his desire to continue playing the game. In my opinion, a sure sign of a bad coach is receiving players with a passion for the game and destroying it beyond repair.

Dr. Goldberg's 20 Characteristics of a Great Coach
(as quoted directly from his article)

1. THE VERY BEST COACHES GET THEIR ATHLETES TO BELIEVE IN THEMSELVES

Good coaches inspire their players to do more than they think they can. In fact, all good teachers do this. They get their students to entertain possibilities that stretch the limits of their beliefs. Part of this involves building the athlete up rather than knocking him down.

Good coaches always build self-esteem rather than undermine it. This self-esteem building is not a gimmick nor is it done artificially. In other words the coach doesn't praise a mediocre effort. He/she simply makes it a practice to catch his/her athletes doing things right. The good coach doesn't get caught up in playing head games that leave the athlete questioning his/her abilities.

2. THE REALLY EFFECTIVE COACHES DO NOT USE EMBARRASSMENT AND HUMILIATION AS "TEACHING TOOLS"

One of the characteristics of really bad coaches is that they regularly use embarrassment and humiliation. They think nothing of calling out or putting down an athlete in front of his/her peers, fans or parents. These coaches mistakenly believe that this is the way that you build character and mental toughness.

What they don't really understand is that these abusive techniques are the most effective way I know to emotionally destroy kids. Embarrassing and humiliating a child/young adult for a failure, mistake or shortcoming is an aggressive assault on that athlete. In fact, when an adult does it, it's called **child abuse** -- no ifs, ands or buts! There is **nothing** educational or constructive about it. It tears down that athlete and grossly undermines his/her self-esteem. It can emotionally scar that child for life! This is **not** how good coaches operate.

3. GREAT COACHES ARE GREAT LIFE TEACHERS

A good coach understands that what he/she is teaching goes far beyond the X's & O's of the court, track or field. As a consequence this kind of individual does not just teach the skills, technique and strategy within the narrow confines of the sport.

Instead he/she looks for opportunities where the more important life lessons can be taught such as mastering hardship, handling and rebounding from failures and setbacks, trusting your teammates, sacrificing individual needs for the benefit of the group, emotionally dealing with winning and losing, good sportsmanship, fair play, honesty, integrity, etc.

4. THE BEST COACHES KEEP THE GAME IN PERSPECTIVE

Somewhat related to #3, the best coaches are able to keep their sport in perspective. They do not get distracted by how big any one game is in relation to their job as a teacher. Similarly, they understand that sports are just games and are merely a vehicle to teach their charges other, more important life lessons.

They understand that what they teach and how they teach it will have an impact on the student that goes far beyond the sport. They know that long after the athlete has put away his bats, balls, racquets and other sport paraphernalia, the effect of his/her relationship with the coach will continue to influence that individual's life and happiness.

Therefore, whenever they coach, no matter how big the game, these coaches keep it all in perspective.

5. GREAT COACHES DO NOT LET THEIR EGOS AND SELF-WORTH GET TIED UP IN THE OUTCOME

The best coaches are psychologically healthy enough to know that they are **not** their performances, regardless of what others around them may say.

They do not feel diminished as an individual when their teams fail nor do they feel that much better about themselves when their squads succeed. These individuals understand that coaching is only one thing of many that they do, and therefore they do not let this one thing solely define themselves as a person.

Coaches who get into trouble with their athletes do so because they are emotionally more vulnerable and tend to feel threatened by a loss or failure. Their egos are on the line whenever these individuals compete, and therefore they feel like they have much more to lose.

If your ego is on the line whenever your team competes, then you will be quite vulnerable to saying and doing some rather unfortunate things with your athletes. Many blatant coaching mistakes come directly from the coach's overemphasis on the game's outcome because that individual self-esteem is too caught up with this outcome.

6. GREAT COACHES UNDERSTAND INDIVIDUAL DIFFERENCES IN THEIR ATHLETES

The best coaches have a basic understanding that each athlete on their team is different in attitude, personality, response-ability, sensitivity and how they handle criticism and adversity.
As a consequence, these coaches take the time to get to know each athlete's individual differences and styles.

They then hand-tailor what they say to and how they treat this athlete to achieve maximum coaching effectiveness. They know that while one athlete may respond well to a hard edge and raised voice, this approach may totally shut another one down.

You can't be really effective with a team full of individuals unless you truly take the time to get to know what works best for each one.

7. THE BEST COACHES COACH THE PERSON, NOT JUST THE ATHLETE

Really effective coaches take the time to get to know the athlete as a person. They take an interest in the athlete's life off the field, court or track. They do not see personal, academic or social problems as a distraction to the job of coaching the athlete. In fact, they view these "outside problems" as an opportunity to further build a relationship with the athlete and help him/her become a better person.

This kind of caring is never lost on the athlete. Coaches who take an interest in the athlete's total life are more trusted and respected than those who don't. Coaches who really care about the athlete as a person are better motivators.

Do **not** approach your athletes' outside problems as outside of your coaching purview. You can't ever separate the athlete as a performer from who he/she is as a person. Relationship issues, family problems, academic stressors and gender issues all of which seem to have no relationship at all to the sport are all importantly related!

If you have an investment in truly being an effective and successful coach and teacher, then these need to be considered by you when they come up.

8. THE BEST COACHES ARE FLEXIBLE

They are flexible in their approach to their teaching, and they are flexible in their approach to their players. For example, when an athlete struggles learning a play or correctly executing a specific technique or strategy, the better coaches do not look at this as a "learning disability" and blame the athlete for their incompetence, thick headedness or ignorance. Instead they approach it as a "teaching disability" and therefore change how they are presenting the material to that athlete.

If one approach doesn't work, then they try another and another until they figure out the best way to reach that particular athlete. Similarly, coaches who take it personally when an athlete has a learning or performance problem are missing the boat. Just because that athlete may not be responding to your coaching does not mean that he/she has an attitude or commitment problem.

Be flexible enough to examine yourself when your athletes struggle. Rigidly assuming that they are the ones with the problem is not the mark of a good coach. Remember, rigidity is not a quality that goes with success and winning.

Coaches who are rigid, who continually adopt the attitude that "it's my way or the highway," are far less effective than those coaches who have mastered the fine art of being flexible. Understand here that flexibility does **not** mean being wishy-washy. You can be flexible and strong at the same time.

9. THE GREAT COACHES ARE GREAT COMMUNICATORS

You can't be effective as a coach unless you can successfully reach the individuals who you are working with. Good coaches understand that communication is a two-way street and involves a back and forth between coach and athlete.
Bad coaches think that communication is a one-way street. You talk and the athletes listen. **Period!**

Instead, effective communication entails that you as a coach carefully listen to what your athletes are saying. When your athletes talk you must **be quiet inside so that you can listen**. Unless you carefully listen to them when they talk, then you won't have a clue as to what your athletes are really saying or how to best help them.

Far too many coaches are too busy countering in their head what their athletes are saying to actually hear them. If you can't learn how to listen, then you will never truly be effective in reaching your players.

10. GOOD COACHES TAKE THE TIME TO LISTEN TO AND EDUCATE THEIR ATHLETES' PARENTS

Many coaches find it a bit of an inconvenience that they have to actually deal with the parents of their athletes. If your job entails having to interact with parents understand this. Your life will be far easier, and you will be much more effective if you make it a regular practice to communicate with the parents and educate them about the sport and the role they need to play on the team.

Your success as a coach often depends upon getting parents to work with you, not against you. The only way to make this happen is if you take the time to talk to and train your parents. This means you must learn to listen to their concerns and questions. Take a proactive role with them. Do **not** wait for a problem or crisis before you decide that it's time to actually approach your parents.

Do so right from the beginning of the season and do it often. Let them know about their support role on the team. Help them understand that their job is **not** to motivate or coach their child.

Teach them what are appropriate and inappropriate behaviors at games and on the sidelines. Educate them about the sport and what it takes to excel. Explain your philosophy about competition and playing time. Be open to feedback in a non-defensive manner.

Never assume that your parents know what they should do and how they should behave. Approach them like your athletes. You coach your athletes. You must also invest some of your time and energy into coaching and training their parents. Be proactive with your parents, not reactive. Use an educational, preventative model when working with them rather than a crisis intervention one.

11. GOOD COACHES "WALK THE TALK" WITH THEIR ATHLETES AND PARENTS

If you want to be effective in reaching those that you coach, then you must learn to put your actions where your mouth is.

That is, there must be some congruence between what you say and how you act. If you are teaching your players about the virtues of consistent, hard work yet you yourself are inconsistent in this area, then what you are really teaching your athletes is that you are a hypocrite, it's really okay to slough off and that talk is cheap.

Because you have decided to coach, you have put yourself in a position of intense public scrutiny. Everyone will always be watching you, even when you think not. As a consequence you must always be sure that whatever comes out of your mouth is closely matched by how you act.

What I'm really saying here is that **your most powerful teaching tool is modeling**. You should operate upon the principle that your actions and how you conduct yourself will always speak much louder than your words. Actively model the behaviors and attitude that you want your players to adopt.

12. GOOD COACHES KEEP THE LEARNING ENVIRONMENT EMOTIONALLY SAFE

There are a lot of social things that go on in sports between teammates that make the learning environment emotionally unsafe: Scapegoating, ostracism, cruelty, emotional and physical abuse, acted out petty jealousies and the list goes on and on.

Many coaches refuse to deal with these "locker room" or "soap opera" issues because they don't necessarily happen on the field, and therefore these coaches claim they have nothing to do with the athlete's or team's performance. Nothing could be further from the truth.

Good coaches understand this basic fact, that the emotional climate on the team is everything and dramatically affects how players practice and perform. Ignoring these "irrelevant and distracting" social issues and letting them continue is like turning your back on an infection and allowing it to fester. In both cases the problem with its resultant pain will only spread and increase in intensity.

Good coaches make it their job to directly and immediately deal with the social garbage that sometimes arises between players. They make it very clear to their athletes which behaviors are appropriate and acceptable when interacting with teammates, and which are not and therefore will not be tolerated.

These coaches give a very clear message to all members of the team that cruelty, petty jealousies and mistreatment of others will not be tolerated and is counter to the mission of the team. As a consequence, this kind of coach creates an atmosphere of safety on the team that is absolutely crucial for optimal learning and peak performance.

13. GREAT COACHES CONTINUALLY CHALLENGE THEIR ATHLETES TO DO BETTER AND PUSH THEIR LIMITS

One way that great coaches inspire their athletes to believe in themselves is by continually putting them in situations that challenge their limiting beliefs. That is, these coaches are always pushing their athletes outside of their comfort zone, physically, mentally and emotionally, and then helping them discover that, in fact, they can do better than they first believed they could.

These coaches teach the "**get comfortable-being uncomfortable principle**." That is, the only way to grow physically and emotionally is to constantly challenge yourself to do things that aren't easy, to attempt things that truly stretch you.

The best coaches do not allow their players to just get by with the status quo. They refuse to tolerate mediocrity in effort, attitude, technique, training or performance. Because they continually challenge their athletes, they are able to keep them highly motivated.

There is nothing more motivating to an athlete than being challenged, experiencing themselves successfully rising to meet that test, and as a result improving.

When coaches fail to adequately challenge their athletes, when they instead allow them to remain stagnating within their comfort zone, they will ultimately end up losing those athletes to boredom and apathy.

14. THE BEST COACHES CONTINUALLY CHALLENGE THEMSELVES

Good coaches practice what they preach. They continually model the attitudes and behaviors that they want their players to adopt. Along these lines, these coaches always maintain a "beginner's mind" when it comes to their professional development within the sport.

Good coaches understand that regardless of how much success they may have had in the past doing things their own way, they can always learn new and better ways of teaching the sport. These coaches are always open to learning the very latest that may be available within their field, be it regarding strategy, technique, conditioning, mental training or motivation.

In this way these coaches continually step out of their comfort zone as "experts" and put themselves in the more uncomfortable position as "beginner and learner."

They are always looking for fresh ideas to spice up and enhance what they are already doing. They attend coaching conferences, read new books, watch and listen to what's current on DVD and CD programs, and actively explore ways of getting the job done better.

These coaches are not rigidly closed-minded nor do they fight what is usually a fast changing technology within their sport. Because these coaches "walk the talk" around being open to new ideas, and demand from their athletes exactly what they demand from themselves, their athletes are far more motivated to meet the coach's higher expectations.

15. THE VERY BEST COACHES ARE PASSIONATE ABOUT WHAT THEY DO

Success in and out of sports very often comes out of a love for what you are doing. The more you love your sport, the better chance that you have of reaching your goals. Passion (love) is a high test fuel that will power you over obstacles, beyond setbacks and through frustration until you achieve success.

As a coach, your passion for the sport and for coaching as a profession is what will ultimately make you a great coach. Passion is infectious and if you approach your practices and competitions with it, soon after your athletes will "catch" it.

Passion in a teacher is motivational. Passion inspires others. It gets them excited and gives them a reason to stretch themselves. Coaches who lack this love for what they do, and who just seem to be going through the motions, directly communicate their lack of enthusiasm to their athletes. Very soon you'll find that their athletes are doing much the same.

As they say, "nothing great was ever achieved without enthusiasm." To be great in your field you must discover your passion for it. If you're bored coaching then you will bore your athletes.

If you can't seem to find the passion in coaching then perhaps it's time that you seriously considered doing something else.

16. GOOD COACHES ARE EMPATHIC AND TUNED INTO THE FEELINGS OF THEIR PLAYERS

Empathy is the ability to tap into another's feeling, experience what they are feeling, and to then communicate your understanding to that other person. When you are empathic you demonstrate the skill of being able to step into another's shoes and walk in them long enough so that you truly can feel what he/she is feeling from his/her model of the world, **not** yours!

Good communicators have this ability. When you are empathic you leave your athlete feeling that you as his/her coach deeply understands. This goes a long way in building athlete loyalty, self-esteem and motivation.

While an insensitive, unfeeling coach can easily sabotage his/her players' confidence and contribute to performance problems, a tuned-in coach can do the exact opposite.

He/she contributes to the athlete's sense of well-being, personal safety, self-confidence and, ultimately, peak performance.

Keep in mind that being empathic doesn't necessarily mean that you are an emotional pushover. You can have the ability to understand where your players are coming from and still make the coaching decisions that you feel are necessary.

Coaches who lack the ability or don't take the time to tune into the emotions of their athletes because they mistakenly believe that "all this emotional crap" is a total waste, end up inadvertently undermining their best coaching efforts.

When you are an emotional "bull in the China shop" with your athletes, routinely tromping all over their feelings you will gradually alienate your players, create team dissension and produce a group of underachieving athletes.

17. GOOD COACHES ARE HONEST AND CONDUCT THEMSELVES WITH INTEGRITY

What else needs to be said about this one? Your most powerful teaching tool as a coach is modeling. How you conduct yourself in relation to your athletes, their parents, your opponents, the referees, the fans and the media is never lost on your players. They see and hear virtually everything that you say and do.

One of the fastest ways of turning your players and everyone else around you off is to model dishonesty and a lack of integrity in some or all of your interactions.

A dishonest coach is one who lacks self-respect and therefore will never earn the respect of others.

Be aware of how you conduct yourself in every aspect of your coaching. Be an honest role model. Demonstrate character and class. These qualities are ultimately far more important in the long run than how many games or championships your teams have won.

19. THE BEST COACHES MAKE THE SPORT FUN FOR THEIR ATHLETES

It doesn't really matter what level you coach at from the pros all the way down to Little League. It doesn't really matter whether a national title is at stake in this particular game or just simply bragging rights around the neighborhood. Sports are just games and games are meant to be fun!

One of your most important jobs as a coach is to find creative ways to integrate this fun into what you do over the course of the season, on a daily basis in practice and during those important competitions. Even if you're coaching at a high level D-I school, one of your tasks is to try to keep your players enjoying that tedious, painful grind.

Fun is the glue that bonds peak and performance together. If your players aren't having fun, they will get much less out of practice. If they get caught up in being too serious in competitions, then they're much more likely to play tightly and tentatively. When an athlete is enjoying him/herself, that athlete is loose and relaxed. Since loose and relaxed are two of the most crucial ingredients to peak performance, it is in your best interests as a coach to find innovative ways to keep your athletes smiling.

Keep in mind that it's perfectly fine for you to make the fun "goal directed." That is, figure out ways within your normal grueling practices to pique your players' funny bone. Periodically and unexpectedly interject the absurd or hilarious.

Just don't get too caught up in how important a particular game or tournament may be. Nothing is that important that you'd want to totally botch it up with an excess of seriousness. And remember, the younger the athletes are that you work with, the more fun you have to weave into your practices.

19. GOOD COACHES ARE NOT DEFENSIVE IN THEIR INTERACTIONS WITH THEIR PLAYERS OR PARENTS

Part of being a good communicator is that you have to be open to negative feedback and criticism. This is not something that is very easy to do, and most of us respond to this kind of negative feedback by getting defensive, closing off and going on the counter attack.

If you want to be successful as a coach you have to learn to be open to all kinds of feedback. You have to train yourself to carefully listen to what others have to say to you and consider their comments and points of view.

You may not necessarily agree with their assessment of you or their feedback, but it's in your best interests as a professional to at least listen.

This is especially important if the comments and negative feedback are coming from your players. Far too many coaches refuse to listen to any complaints or criticisms from their athletes, categorically dismissing them as whining. Unfortunately this is like throwing out the baby with the bath water.

Sometimes the negative feedback and complaints that come from your athletes hold the seeds to you becoming a better, more successful coach. Put the defensive stance away. It's unbecoming and ultimately counterproductive.

20. GREAT COACHES USE THEIR ATHLETES' MISTAKES AND FAILURES AS VALUABLE TEACHING OPPORTUNITIES

One of the bigger teaching mistakes that coaches make is to get angry and impatient with their athletes when they mess-up or fail. This response to your athletes' mistakes will ensure that they will make plenty more of them.

Coaches who consistently yell at their players for screwing up end up making them too nervous to play to their potential.

Furthermore, knowing that your coach gets impatient and angry when you make mistakes will cause a player to worry about this while he's performing. An athlete who's afraid of messing up during performance is an athlete who will always play tight and tentatively.

Good coaches know that mistakes and failures are the necessary prerequisites to learning, improvement and, therefore success.

Therefore when an athlete makes a mistake, they do not go ballistic on the sidelines. They do **not** want to teach their athletes to be afraid of making mistakes. They do not want their athletes distracted by fear. Good coaches know that an athlete needs to be relaxed and loose in order to play well, and that a fear of making mistakes always undermines this relaxed state.

To this end, the good coaches give their athletes permission to fail and make mistakes. They instill in their players the understanding that mistakes and failures are nothing more than feedback about what you did wrong and specifically what you need to do differently next time.

The best coaches teach that failure is feedback and feedback is the **breakfast of champions**!

A Positive Influence

"To be as good as it can be, a team has to buy into what you as the coach are doing. They have to feel you're a part of them and they're a part of you."
~Bobby Knight

Years ago after a new high school was built, many of our players ended up living within the new boundary instead of the one they had previously played in, which created an instant rivalry between our high school and the new one.

Though most of the players decided to attend the new school, there were a few that chose to remain at ours.

Our two schools were invited to participate in a special Saturday of football at the University of Utah's Rice Eccles Stadium. There were four teams invited to play that day, and we were paired against our new rival. The game provided all of the excitement of a closely fought game. When it came down to the last play of the game, it was devastating when the other team scored and we lost.

When our team's coaches met back at the school licking our wounds from the loss, a few of the players came in to speak to us about the game. One of them, who resided within the new high school boundary, had elected to remain at our school.

With all of the emotion of a player who had just suffered a devastating loss, he walked over to our head coach, coach Miller and said, "Even if we never beat them, I'm still glad I stayed here to play for you."

That one simple, profound statement was the result of a coach who had become a positive influence for his team. I will forever remember that inspiring moment.

For far too many coaches the need to win becomes all too important to the detriment of the players, and their ego can get in the way of a satisfying experience.

Don't get me wrong -- I despise losing as I'm very passionate about my team's success. I have a hard time sleeping for a few days if they lose, and it's even worse if they lose to a rival team.

However, the bottom line still remains that as a coach the game should never be about you, but rather about the players you're responsible for.

While coaching my daughter's basketball team of 13-year-old girls, we concluded the season paired against our rival team in the championship game. Having not lost any games during the entire season, we entered the game with great confidence.

During the process of the game it became obvious to all in attendance that the officials favored the other team. While later talking to some of the parents from the other team, they expressed how bad they felt for our girls due to the one-sided officiating.

One parent stated "Your girls were just cheated out of a fair game." I was very vocal during the game regarding the way the game was being officiated. When the final buzzer sounded, we were trailing by three points and lost the championship game.

My first inclination was to run to the officials and tell them exactly what I thought about their officiating. I stopped short when I remembered the game wasn't about me but my players, so I congratulated the other team and swallowed my pride. It wasn't easy, but it was the right thing to do.

Headline: "Utah High School Football Coach Suspends Entire Team to Build Character"

In September of 2013, Matt Labrum -- the head football coach of Union High School in Roosevelt, Utah -- suspended the entire team to teach them a lesson on character.

"We felt like everything was going in a direction that we didn't want our young men going," he said, following the suspension of all forty-one players on the team. Having coached the team for only two years, Labrum recognized that as a coaching staff they needed to change the path of some of their players.

Some of the players had been accused of negative behavior such as cyberbullying and skipping class. Even though their involvement was inconclusive, the thought of his players having done these things was enough for him to take action. Coach Labrum recognized his responsibility to the team, and took this opportunity to teach his young players to be accountable for their actions and grow into responsible men.

Following a game where Union High School lost against Judge Memorial, Coach Labrum and the rest of the coaching staff determined it was time to take a stand. In the locker room following the game, Labrum informed the team that due to the off-field behavior by some team members the entire team was suspended, and they all needed to turn in their equipment.

The players were then informed there'd be a meeting the following Saturday at seven in the morning to discuss how they could earn their way back onto the team.

"We felt like we needed to make a stand," Labrum said. "We looked at it as a chance to say, 'Hey, we need to focus on some other things that are more important than winning a football game'."

The next day during the team meeting he gave the suspended players a letter titled "Union Football Character," which was basically a pep talk regarding the path back to becoming a better player. The requirements included community service, attending study hall, and attending all classes.

Students with poor grades were required to show improvement, perform service at home, and were to report what they had done back to the coaching staff.

The text from the actual letter is as follows:

> Gentlemen, we are not pleased with how our football brothers are representing our family, school, community, alumni, family and yourselves. It is a privilege to play this wonderful game! We must earn the opportunity, to have the honor to put on our high schools jersey each Thursday and Friday night!
>
> The lack of character we are showing off the field is outshining what we are achieving on the field.
>
> We want student-athletes that are humble to learn and grow through adversity and success on and off the field. We want a team that others want to associate themselves with and support; winning isn't the most important criteria for that to happen.
>
> Humbleness, thankfulness, humility, respect, courage and honor are much more important than winning ballgames! We can achieve both if we start to act with others' feelings in mind and focus on how we can make someone else's day instead of just wrapped up in ourselves.
>
> WHEN WE ARE WORKING ON THIS AND ACHIEVING THIS WE WILL BE MOLDING OUR CHARACTER IN A POSITIVE WAY!
>
> Right now we are way off as a collective group. We want change and are going to make changes now.
>
> As of tonight we are no longer playing football until we meet certain criteria!
>
> TURN YOUR JERSEYS IN NOW!
>
> Saturday: 7:00 a.m. electing captains "Attitude Reflects Leadership" -- Remember the Titans.

Monday: 3:30 we will be doing a service project during practice time, come prepared to work, then we are all required to attend the Cougar Legend Banquet. Find ways to serve during this event.

Tuesday: We will be performing more service in lieu of practice.

Wednesday: Study Hall begins at 3:30 and we better have specific items to work on.

We will be in there for the duration of practice. You must have enough work for 2 hours.

Criteria to EARN jersey back for Friday's Game:

1) Attend all practices that we have planned and any others that may come up.
2) Be on time and totally prepared.
3) No F's or discipline problems.
4) Do an individual service project for your family, give me a typed report of it and pictures, and have your parents sign it. (Due Wed. before study hall.)
5) Memorize and pass this quote off to one of the coaches at some point during study hall:

"Good character is more to be praised than outstanding talent. Most talents are, to some extent, a gift. Good character, by contrast is not given to us. We have to build it, piece by piece -- by thought, by choice, courage, and determination."

If you meet ALL criteria by Wednesday night, you will have earned the privilege to play in the games on Thursday and Friday. If you fail then you will miss this week's game.

Signed,
Your Coaches

Coach Labrum's actions received the full support of the high school administration as well as all of the parents who had sons on the team.

Coach John Wooden

"Success is peace of mind which is a direct result of self-satisfaction in knowing you did your best to become the best you are capable of becoming."
~John Wooden, Basketball Coach

Coach Wooden -- perhaps one the finest college basketball coaches the sporting world has ever seen -- coached the UCLA team to ten NCAA championships (that included seven consecutive championships). His team won eighty-eight straight games, which no other basketball coach has come close to accomplishing.

As much as he was a great coach on the court, Wooden was much more off the court to his players as the environment he created around his team was one of respect, character, and honor.

Playing for Coach Wooden meant playing by his rules: Never score without acknowledging a teammate, treat your opponent with respect, and one word of profanity and you're done for the day. "Never lie, never cheat, never steal," Wooden would say. "Earn the right to be proud and confident."

Discipline was also a standard Wooden demanded from his players. "Discipline yourself, and others won't need to." One of his rules was that the players weren't allowed to have long hair or facial hair.

When All-American center, Bill Walton, showed up one day with a full beard he said emphatically, "It's my right." When Wooden asked him if he really felt that strongly about his right, Walton replied "Yes." Wooden responded with "That's good, Bill. I admire people who have strong beliefs and stick by them -- I really do. We're going to miss you."

Walton immediately shaved his beard.

Through his love of the game and for his players, Coach Wooden established lifelong relationships. There were a total of 180 players that played for him during his career.

He knew where 172 of them were after they graduated, and many stayed in close contact with their coach until the day he passed away in 2010. John Wooden is a perfect example of the positive influence a coach is capable of having with his players.

A Not So Positive Influence

"Be more concerned with your character than your reputation. Because your character is what you really are, while your reputation is merely what others think you are."
~John Wooden

If you've been involved in sports at any level, you've probably witnessed coaches having a negative influence on their players. It's a tragedy when this occurs.

We've all heard the stories of coaches losing their tempers, and possibly witnessed it in person. Abuse of another human being is never acceptable in or out of sports, and should not be tolerated at any level. Far too often destructive behavior is ignored because the coach has a winning team.

For instance, when legendary Indiana University (Hoosiers) coach Bobby Knight threw a chair onto the basketball court following a foul being called on one of his players and a technical foul on himself, as out of control as his actions were he felt his anger was justifiable in support of his player.

Unfortunately, Knight had many alleged issues of abusing players. Indiana University's President Miles Brand placed a zero tolerance policy on him after receiving such reports.

In September, 2000, he was summarily dismissed as their head coach for grabbing freshman Kent Harvey's arm.

In 2009, when the university inducted Coach Knight into their Hall of Fame, he was a no-show.

I would therefore assert there's a difference between anger ***in support of*** your players, and anger ***directed at*** your players. Good coaches know never to approach or cross the line between abuse and passion.

Leave Your Ego at the Door

"When you walk through those doors, (team weight room) leave your pride and ego outside. A humble man is a teachable man."
~Coach Mike Miller (directed at both his players and the entire coaching staff)

Having been involved in multiple sports for the last thirteen years, I've witnessed coaches who sit on the bench, or stand on the sideline and act more like a spectator than a coach, or even abusive coaches. For years I watched one who had such a big ego that he failed to see the damage he caused to his players.

So How Do You Know if Your Coach is a Bad Coach?

The first thing to consider is does the coach put the players' needs and success above his or her own? Is the game about them or the team? It doesn't take long to recognize a coach who isn't in the game for the team. They almost always blame the players for the team's failure, but are quick to take credit for their success. They typically never take responsibility for their actions, and fail to see the success possible even in a loss.

To only teach X's and O's to my athletes would be a failure on my part. The mental and emotional aspects of the game are just as important, if not more so, than the physical aspect.

Great coaches are able to manage all three, whereas bad coaches tend to fall short with the mental and emotional side of the game. The X's and O's are fairly easy to teach; it's knowing how to build up every athlete on the team that takes skill and talent.

I believe coaches promoting their athletes to the next level has become a lost art because they lose sight of their responsibility to them. However, if a coach is 100% invested in their players, promoting them to the next level comes naturally.

As a coach of an AAU team my job is to teach every aspect of the game to my players, and to get them prepared for the next level.

When I coached my daughter's eighth grade basketball team, every practice and game was managed with the intention of preparing them for high school basketball. (Many great coaches had been involved in preparing them, so I can't take all the credit for their success.)

All eight players made high school teams, and four made their JV-Varsity teams as a freshman, including my daughter. Those that made the sophomore team all dressed for and play in their JV game.

My approach is the same as a high school football coach. I prepare the kids to not only compete at the high school level, but to go on to play in college. Obviously not all eighth graders will make the high school team, and not all high school players will play in college.

As an AAU coach that's not for me to decide. My job is to prepare and promote them the best I can with the talent they have; the rest is up to them and the recruiters.

I once had a conversation with a player from our local high school basketball team following a humiliating defeat. When I asked him what happened, his answer was that the team wasn't prepared for the game. Thinking about what he said, he backtracked and followed it with, "We didn't execute the coaches' game plan, and the coaches were pissed." Having watched the game, there was no question his first response was the most honest.

Why did he alter his comment? I believe he thought if it were to get back to his coach he'd risk losing game time and being cut the next year. To me, having that kind of fear is a red flag his coach was failing him.

I watched this same coach cut or run off some of his best players, and stifle the talent of the "superstars" remaining on his team. Having had a real superstar on his team early in his career who took the spotlight off him, he seemed to be determined not allow it to happen again.

During games, the father of this "superstar" would keep stats on his son. When the coach informed the players their parents were no longer allowed to keep statistics on them, I wondered why he felt he had the right to do that.

However, following his announcement, the superstar's father brought a large whiteboard to the games to keep stats on his son and to let the coach know he wasn't intimidated by his demands.

Following a season where his team failed to make the state tournament, this same coach told his players they weren't allowed to play with any other teams during the off-season. Again I asked myself, what kind of coach would think they had the right to demand that from his players? Was he looking out for them or himself? Looking back, I believe his actions were based on his players playing better for other coaches which in turn made him look bad.

"Great coaches know their team is only as strong as its weakest player and works hard to give every player the chance to improve his or her skills."
~USA Hockey Magazine

A few years ago I attended a high school basketball game where a local school was paired against a nationally ranked team. I sat next to parents of one of the boys from the ranked school, and we chatted about their team's success.

After the game started, it became obvious players from our local school were hesitant to shoot the ball. When one of the parents asked me why I thought they were afraid, I suggested it was possible the coach wasn't allowing them to.

Utah high school basketball doesn't have a shot clock, so our team's strategy was to hold the ball at half court and run the clock. The halftime score was 20 to 6 for the ranked team. Following the game, the players of our local team said their coaches were pleased they'd only lost by 19 points instead of 30 when they'd previously played against the ranked team.

I'd never seen a more blatant message that our coach didn't believe in his team. While some coaches may call it a strategy, I called it "tail firmly placed between the legs." In my estimation, if you're not going to come out swinging why come out at all?

Coaches fail their players by telling them they're not allowed to play rather than teaching them the correct skills to compete. It shows lack of character by giving up on a player or a team. Sadly there are many of these types of individuals coaching at the high school level where they ignore their coaching responsibilities.

If a player has been in your program for three or four years and hasn't been allowed to shoot the ball, you've failed them as a coach. Your job is to teach the game and build their confidence, but if you can't achieve that then you shouldn't coach.

Being Hard on Players

There's a huge difference between being tough or being mean and cruel on players. I'm of the opinion that at times it's necessary for a coach to be hard on a player. However, shouting during the process of coaching and instruction is much different than yelling at a player and telling them how bad they are (especially in front of other teammates).

This may sound like I'm splitting hairs, but it's really about how the player feels after being yelled at. Do they feel they've learned something from their coach? Or did the coach make them feel like they're a bad player and they lose their drive to play?

I love how my daughter's coach coaches his players. He has a lot of passion for the game, and it's clear he places his players first. Every time he yells at one of his players or the team as a whole, he immediately rebuilds their confidence with a pat on the head or an encouraging comment.

While patting her on the head, he told my daughter, "I'm hard on you because I know you can handle it." Apparently he's a coach who understands and manages the responsibility of coaching each player quite well.

I once heard of a coach who called a time out and shouted at his son in front of the other eighth grade players. Even though the game still had a long time before the final buzzer, he told his son to sit on the bench and take off his shoes because he was done playing. Later in the game he again yelled at his son and demanded he go wait in the car.

(Unfortunately, this coach is affiliated with one of our local high schools, and in my opinion should never be allowed to coach any sport now or ever.)

You Get What You Coach

National Basketball League players make turnovers. Major League Baseball players that hit the ball only 33% of the time still get paid millions of dollars. National Football League quarterbacks throw interceptions, and running backs fumble the ball. But in youth leagues from high school to college and on to professional leagues, instructing players how to correct their mistakes is also becoming a lost art.

During my oldest daughter's sophomore season at her high school, they developed a playoff of the tipped ball in which they usually scored. The player jumping would tip the ball to my daughter, then she'd pass it to a teammate streaking toward the basket that usually culminated in an open layup.

During one game she made a bad pass that resulted in a turnover. Less than five seconds into the game the coach yanked her out. Making mistakes is part of playing the game. So removing a player because of one or two mistakes instills the fear of playing, and is counterproductive as it sets them up for future mistakes.

I'm impressed with coaches who pulls a player because they're making mistakes, coaches them up, then immediately or soon after gets them back into the game. Even if the coach's style is considered passionate education (yelling), the players learn how not to make the same mistakes and go back into the game to play even better.

As coaches we sometimes complain about our teams' game performance. Unfortunately, I used to be one of those coaches. One day I and a few other coaches were sitting in Coach Miller's office following a devastating defeat discussing our players' failures during the game. When he entered the office, and quickly assessed the subject of our conversation, he immediately corrected us by stating, "What you got out of your players during that game is exactly what you coached."

His simple statement instilled within me that as a coach I am solely responsible for my players' performance. So if I want better performances, I had to do a better job coaching.

Coaches in Youth Tackle Football

As it relates to youth tackle football, coaches play a critical role. In my opinion this is where the leagues running the programs fail to teach the coaches how to coach.

I certainly don't know everything, but I've learned a great deal during my years of coaching. As players come into the program, I instantly recognize bad habits that need to be corrected.

Youth coaches who haven't received proper training (or don't go out of their way to get it) don't have the knowledge or instincts to identify then fix habits before they get out of hand.

Requiring coaches to learn how to teach proper tackling techniques and drills would reduce injuries. For example, in the past teams would run a tackling drill at the end of practice called "Bull in the Ring" where players would form a circle with one player standing in the middle. The coaches would either tap a player or call out a name of a player in the circle; then the player would run full speed to tackle the player standing in the middle of the circle.

As you can imagine, a circle with 20 to 25 players tends to be pretty large, so repeatedly running at full speed to impact creates a high possibility for injury. Fortunately, this drill is no longer allowed by many leagues.

There are other impact drills that in the past would have players lined up 10 to 15 yards apart and run to impact. Our local league now requires the players to be within five yards of each other for any tackling drill.

Coaches should be taught proper head placement at impact, as it not only assists in a proper tackle but helps in preventing concussions. The NFL has begun to place more importance on this by way of a 15-yard penalty if a player leads with their head at impact.

I mentioned earlier that Chris Carter said, "Our best coaches are coaching our best players, and that's in professional football. Our worst coaches are coaching the most critical position, and that is the 9, 10, 11 year-old people."

This statement -- along with the statistic that 70% of the players in America are in the youth programs -- is in my opinion the greatest problem with tackle football. Coaches lacking the proper education to competently teach proper techniques leads to unnecessary injuries. Therefore, many injuries could have been prevented with proper coaching.

The responsibility falls on us as parents (yes, that includes me) to put the time and effort into becoming educated on proper techniques. We can no longer sit on the sidelines at games and think we're doing our part to support our children.

If you're going to allow your youngster to play tackle football, then you must accept the responsibility to prepare them to play. You never know, you may find a great passion in teaching football and become a well-informed coach and teach others the proper way to play safely.

CHAPTER FOUR

CONCUSSIONS AND NON-CONCUSSION INJURIES

"This overall approach and the specific techniques within the program are exactly the next steps we need to take to improve head safety in tackle football. The effort to teach effective, yet safe tackling and blocking techniques at the earliest youth levels can only have positive downstream benefits for our players at the high school, college and professional levels."
~Dr. Gerard A. Gioia, Pediatric Neuropsychologist, Division of Pediatric Neuropsychology Chief, Children's National Medical Center; Associate Professor, Departments of Pediatrics and Psychiatry, George Washington University School of Medicine

You may have heard about professional players who were forced into early retirement due to the many concussions they suffered.

I recall watching Steve Young (quarterback for the San Francisco 49ers) on the sideline as one of his teammates was explaining to him what had happened.

Knowing his competitive nature, his teammates hid his helmet to keep him out of the game. The camera followed him on the sidelines while he looked for his helmet and asked his teammates if they knew where it was.

In a CBS News report in relation to a game on January 9, 1999, at the Georgia Dome in Atlanta, "Young was plagued by concussions throughout his career. Officially, Young had suffered seven concussions, but many believe the number to be higher." When Hall of Fame Steve Young retired early due to his many concussions, holding many NFL records he was one of the top rated quarterbacks the League had ever seen.

Study of Head Impacts

There are an estimated five million football players in the United States. The NFL accounts for approximately 2,000; college football approximately 100,000; high school football approximately 1.3 million; and an estimated 3.5 million are accounted for in youth football.

In 2012, Virginia Tech and Wake Forest University released the results of their research on head impacts with youth football players:

> "The manuscript includes the details of over 700 head impacts measured on 7- and 8-year old youth football players. Based on the importance of this initial publication, the School of Biomedical Engineering and Sciences is also announcing a new study to instrument and map the head impact exposure of youth football players for all age groups from 6 years through 18 years. This program will consist of over 240 instrumented helmets on six different football teams in Virginia and North Carolina.
>
> Called the Kinematics of Impact Data Set (KIDS), it is anticipated that this research program will greatly enhance the understanding of child brain biomechanics, and will lead to improvements in youth practice and game techniques as well as the development of improved helmets specifically designed for children. The study is the first of its kind to look at the full age spectrum from age 6 to 18.

> As part of the KIDS study, each team will receive new helmets and new sensors fitted inside the helmet. Each time a player impacts his head, data are recorded and wirelessly downloaded to a computer on the sideline.
>
> The technology is similar to what Virginia Tech has used since 2003 to instrument its collegiate football team. The research conducted with the Virginia Tech football team has led to a better understanding of head impacts in football and how they relate to concussions. Furthermore, this research has led to the development of the National Impact Database, containing the first safety rating system ever available for adult football helmets (STAR Evaluation System)."

According to Stefan Duma (Virginia Tech's professor of biomedical engineering; and department head of the Virginia Tech/Wake Forest University School of Biomedical Engineering and Sciences who directed this project), "In 2011 we collected the first data on one team of youth football players. This new study for 2012 allows for dramatically increased sample size and head exposure mapping for all age groups."

What is a Concussion?

An obvious sign of a concussion is loss of short-term memory (when my son experienced his concussion, he had no memory of what had happened).

According to the Centers for Disease Control and Prevention (CDC), "A concussion is a type of traumatic brain injury, or TBI, caused by a bump, blow, or jolt to the head that can change the way your brain normally works.

Concussions can also occur from a blow to the body that causes the head to move rapidly back and forth. Even a 'ding', 'getting your bell rung', or what seems to be a mild bump or blow to the head can be serious."

Some symptoms include memory loss, irritability, an inability to mentally focus, headaches, depression, and sleep disorder. The CDC has compiled the two charts below to assist in assessing if a person has a concussion:

Signs of a Concussion

As a whole, tackle football programs have made tremendous strides toward not only improving the education surrounding concussions, but the immediate treatment if a concussion is suspected.

As a coach the training I received is simple: If a concussion is suspected, immediately remove the player from the game and don't allow them to return to physical activity related to the sport (i.e., any type of contact drills or games) without a physician's approval.

If a player has incurred a concussion, the key to recovery is to avoid physical contact and lots of rest. It's believed by many professionals that once a concussion occurs, the threshold for another concussion is lessened. It's also believed that following a concussion and during the recovery period any subsequent concussions would be far more damaging than the initial injury. Therefore, education is essential in preventing, treating and clearing a player who has received a concussion.

There's much that coaches and parents can do to help prevent initial and future concussions. Education on the proper technique for tackling as well as any point of contact between players is a great place to start. But learning exercises to strengthen neck muscles is critical to preventing or minimizing a concussion, as the added strength provides support to the head during contact that prevents the brain from slamming back and forth against the skull. Prior to any practice or game where contact is expected, proper stretching of the neck as well as all areas of the body goes a long way toward preventing all types of injuries.

Treating and clearing a player suspected of or has experienced a concussion must be done via a doctor who's had experience with treating concussions. In my son's case it took weeks before a doctor would clear him for contact. To a young player and even his parents this may be difficult to accept due to the fact the injury isn't visible, and the symptoms can dissipate soon after the injury.

Allowing a player to return to contact too soon can be devastating (and possibly permanently debilitating) if they were to receive a blow to the head or body that caused another concussion. It was much easier for me as a parent as well as my son to accept he couldn't play when he broke his collarbone because he was in a sling for over a week, and experienced pain and discomfort for three to four weeks. However, within a few days following his concussion he felt fine, and couldn't understand why he wasn't being returned to active status.

As discussed previously, following a concussion the threshold for subsequent concussions is much lower, which makes it easier to experience the next concussion. Even though the symptoms may have disappeared, it's critical the player receive the needed amount of time away from any bodily contact to fully recover.

Signs Observed by Coaching Staff

- Appears dazed or stunned
- Is confused about assignment or position
- Forgets an instruction
- Is unsure of game, score, or opponent
- Moves clumsily
- Answers questions slowly
- Loses consciousness (*even briefly*)
- Shows mood, behavior, or personality changes
- Can't recall events *prior* to and/or *after* hit or fall

Symptoms Reported by Athletes

- Headache or "pressure" in head
- Nausea or vomiting
- Balance problems or dizziness
- Double or blurry vision
- Sensitivity to light
- Sensitivity to noise
- Feeling sluggish, hazy, foggy, or groggy
- Concentration or memory problems
- Confusion
- Does not "feel right" or is "feeling down"

Non-Concussion Injuries

In February of 2012, USA Football commissioned a scientific study to determine the health and safety of youth football, which included ten youth football leagues in many different states spanning the 2012 and 2013 football seasons.

Their initial report for the 2012 football season was released in 2013, and included tracking injuries from more than 60,000 youth players' events during practice or games for 2,000 athletes of all ages. The following is a sample of the initial findings:

- More than 90% of the 1,913 youth players did not suffer an injury that restricted participation. Fewer than 10% of players incurred an injury, and of those injuries 64% were minor where athletes returned to play on the same day.

- Contusions were the most common injuries (35%), followed by ligament sprains (15%).

- Fewer than 4% of the youth players sustained a concussion.

- Similar to other levels of football, youth football players were more likely to be injured during games than practices.

- No catastrophic head, neck or heat-related injuries were reported.

As you can see, from at least the initial findings relative to the number of athletes participating there were very few injuries, and concussions accounted for fewer than 4% of the injuries. (The full report from USA Football spanning the 2012 and 2013 football season is due to be released in 2014.)

> "We need more studies like this across all of youth sports," said Dr. Patrick Kersey, USA Football Medical Director who is also a physician for Indianapolis-based St. Vincent Sports Performance, a member of numerous medical associations including the American Medical Society for Sports Medicine and the American College of Sports Medicine.
>
> Such a commitment to research is how we advance player safety, determine best practices and continue football's evolution, which has always been part of the game's legacy. Our hope is that more sports will take similar steps for their young athletes."

CHAPTER FIVE

USA FOOTBALL "HEADS UP FOOTBALL"

"Heads Up Football is USA Football's national initiative to help make the sport of football better and safer. A comprehensive collection of resources, programs, applications and promotions to create change and address the complex challenges of player health and safety in youth and high school football."
~usafootball.com

USA Football (URL in References) has made tremendous strides in improving the safety of youth football.

Their Heads Up Football program, which is endorsed by the NFL as well as the NCAA, is a powerful tool for parents and coaches.

The key components of this program are:

- Education and Certification
- Equipment Fitting
- Concussion Recognition and Awareness
- Heat and Hydration
- Heads Up Tackling

Education and Certification

"Only allow your child to play when you know that USA Football certification is there for the coach, and you know that your child is being taught the proper fundamentals of the game and that real intelligence has gone into the preparation of practices."

~Tom Coughlin, Head Coach, New York Giants, www.usafootball.com

USA Football's education and certification is reportedly the only nationally accredited course available. The training content was created by football experts as well as health professionals.

"Give your coaches the best in coaching education. After completing an age-based course, coaches will earn certification."

~usafootball.com

Learning proper tackling technique as a football coach is critical. The Heads Up Football program will provide the training you as a coach or a parent will need to make tackle football safer. As a member of USA Football I strongly recommend that all youth programs and administrators require all their coaches go through the training and earn the certificates offered by Heads Up Football.

Equipment Fitting

"It is essential that every player has a properly fitted helmet and shoulder pads. League administrators, coaches and parents should be able to recognize equipment that fits properly and check the fit of equipment throughout the season. Improperly fitted equipment can place an athlete at greater risk for injury."

~usafootball.com

A properly fitted helmet substantially reduces the risk of sustaining a concussion. As discussed in the chapter on Concussions, it's believed that many are caused by the second impact to the head (meaning that many concussions likely don't occur during the initial impact. But many concussions do occur when the head snaps back from the initial impact.)

Imagine the increased risk of concussions a player's helmet is too loose. Improperly fitted head gear will negate the many advances technology has made in the prevention of concussions.

Concussion Recognition and Awareness

The following is the CDC/USA Football concussion clipboard sticker from usafootball.com that covers the signs and symptoms as well as an action plan for dealing with concussions or the possibility of a concussion:

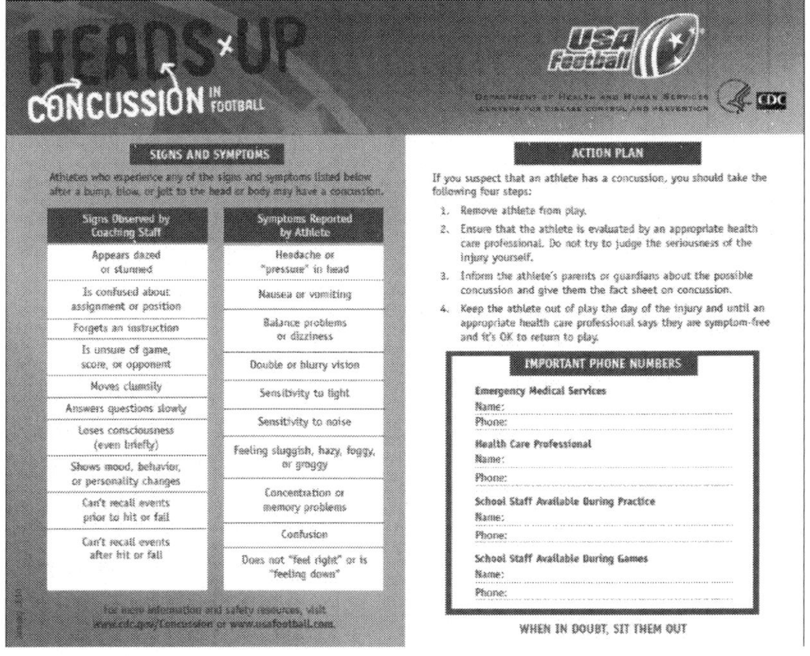

HEADS UP
CONCUSSION IN FOOTBALL

USA Football

Department of Health and Human Services
Centers for Disease Control and Prevention
CDC

SIGNS AND SYMPTOMS

Athletes who experience any of the signs and symptoms listed below after a bump, blow, or jolt to the head or body may have a concussion.

Signs Observed by Coaching Staff

- Appears dazed or stunned
- Is confused about assignment or position
- Forgets an instruction
- Is unsure of game, score, or opponent
- Moves clumsily
- Answers questions slowly
- Loses consciousness (even briefly)
- Shows mood, behavior, or personality changes
- Can't recall events prior to hit or fall
- Can't recall events after hit or fall

Symptoms Reported by Athlete

- Headache or "pressure" in head
- Nausea or vomiting
- Balance problems or dizziness
- Double or blurry vision
- Sensitivity to light
- Sensitivity to noise
- Feeling sluggish, hazy, foggy, or groggy
- Concentration or memory problems
- Confusion
- Does not "feel right" or is "feeling down"

For more information and safety resources, visit www.cdc.gov/Concussion or www.usafootball.com.

ACTION PLAN

If you suspect that an athlete has a concussion, you should take the following four steps:

1. Remove athlete from play.
2. Ensure that the athlete is evaluated by an appropriate health care professional. Do not try to judge the seriousness of the injury yourself.
3. Inform the athlete's parents or guardians about the possible concussion and give them the fact sheet on concussion.
4. Keep the athlete out of play the day of the injury and until an appropriate health care professional says they are symptom-free and it's OK to return to play.

IMPORTANT PHONE NUMBERS

Emergency Medical Services
Name:
Phone:

Health Care Professional
Name:
Phone:

School Staff Available During Practice
Name:
Phone:

School Staff Available During Games
Name:
Phone:

WHEN IN DOUBT, SIT THEM OUT

Heat and Hydration

"The environment, equipment and intensity can place athletes at risk of heat illness. Heat illnesses represent conditions resulting from heat stress, which can be imposed by a number of factors but usually result from the environment or the body creating this heat load itself. Heat illnesses can range from minor to severe, and in particular, exertional heat stroke is a life-threatening emergency."

Heat acclimation awareness has recently driven the implementation of new restrictions on high school football practices. However, it's still working its way down to the pre-high school leagues.

The following is information from the USA Football website regarding acclimation recommendations and suggested practice schedules:

Heat Acclimatization

Use the model below to get youth players acclimated to the heat:

The following are important for understanding the heat acclimatization model:

- Use good judgment. The times listed below are maximum practice times as you acclimate to the heat. Conditions may warrant shorter practice times and intensity.

- Practice is defined as time on the football field (including warm-up, stretching, break time, cool down and any conditioning time).

- These guidelines call for a two-week period (10-14 days) when coaches gradually increase the length of practice and the amount of equipment that can be worn.

- At no time throughout the preseason or regular season should teams practice more than once per day (no two-a-day practices). Teams should be allowed to practice a maximum of four times per week during the preseason.

Heat acclimatization days should be continuous as possible, meaning few days off. However, if your practice schedule is only a few days a week, then remember that the days between your practices (the days off) do not count toward acclimatization days. It will take longer to acclimatize in situations such as this.

Practice Days 1-2

Practices permitted per day: 1
Equipment: Helmets only
Max duration of single practice session: 2 hours
Permitted walkthrough time (not included as practice time): 1 hour (but must be separated from practice for 3 continuous hours).
Contact: Air and Bags (no player-to-player contact)

Practice Days 3-4

Practices permitted per day: 1
Equipment: Helmets and shoulder pads
Max duration of single practice session: 2 hours
Contact: Air, Bags, Control (no full contact)

Practice Days 5-6

Practices permitted per day: 1
Equipment: Full equipment
Max duration of single practice session: 2 hours
Contact: Air, Bags, Control, Thud, Live Action (limit full contact- Thud and Live- to 30 minutes per day)

Heads Up Tackling

USA Football breaks down their tackling fundamentals into five sections.

1. Breakdown Position: The foundation starting point for all movements and drills.

2. Buzzing the Feet: Technique for coming to balance and regaining breakdown position prior to contact.

3. Hit Position: Correct body posture at moment of impact for safer tackling. Head and eyes are up, using the front of shoulder as point of contact.

4. The Shoot: The opening of the hips to generate power and create an ascending tackle.

5. Rip: With head to the side and away from contact, throw double uppercuts and "grab cloth" on the back of the jersey to secure tackle

I recommend USA Football to coaches, parents and athletes as it's a tremendous resource for education and preparation in all aspects of tackle football.

CHAPTER SIX

INTERVIEW WITH CONNIE JONES CERTIFIED ATHLETIC TRAINER

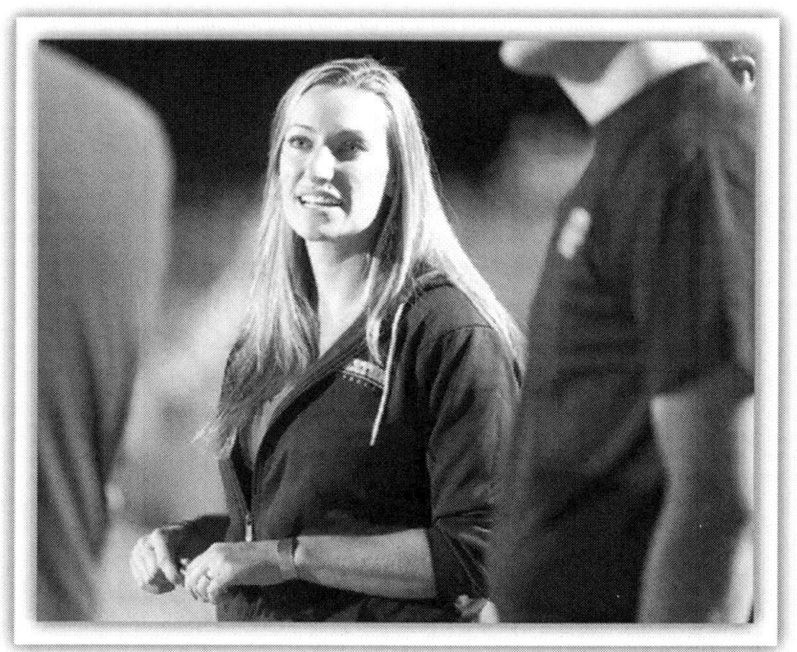

After graduating from high school, Connie Jones had her mind set on being a dentist. However, while attending dental school she realized she didn't want an office job that would keep her inside all day.

Following graduation from the University of Utah with a Bachelor's degree in Athletic Training, she began working as a Registered Physical Therapist (RPT provides athletic trainers to many high schools).

She's currently working on an exercise-based strength and conditioning (CSCS) certification that's over and above the required 50 hours of training and education she's required to complete every two years as part of her continuing education.

During the morning hours she's at the RPT office working with patients suffering from injuries ranging from car crashes to simple overuse. In the afternoons she makes her way over to the high school where she's the athletic trainer for most sports. And at least during the summer and fall months, you'll find her on the Riverton High School, Utah football field.

Her responsibilities include preparing athletes to compete with sophisticated taping, determining their clearance to compete following injury, and being available the moment an injury occurs. Connie also has the authority to sit a player out if she believes they haven't adequately healed following an injury.

When posed with the statement that soccer produced a greater number of injuries than football, she responded with "I absolutely agree."

She quickly followed it with the simple but critical qualification of "But it depends on what you count as an injury. An injury is something that will hold you out of play for an extended period of time. In football you'll see more bumps and bruises and sprained fingers and overuse of things. But in soccer you see more ACLs, more concussions, more MCLs and severely sprained ankles."

The most common injuries Connie treats high school athletes for are Patellar dislocations and tendinitis, and knee injuries which in her opinion are the number one injury.

Connie believes concussions are probably second or third. In 2013 she only treated one concussion, whereas in 2014 she treated six or seven -- four of which were football, two for soccer, and one for dance.

While discussing USA Football's Heads Up Football program with Connie, she disclosed she hadn't been through their program since as a Certified Athletic Trainer (CAT) she's not required to do so to become certified. She is, however, very familiar with their specifications and protocols, and noted that RPT follows some but not all of the protocol outlined in the program.

Explaining to Connie that to become a certified coach or administrator of the USA Heads Up Football program requires about one-and-one-half hours of training.

I asked her if in her opinion that was sufficient time for a coach to learn how to teach proper tackling techniques as well as how to recognize a concussion:

> "With the protocols, yes. I don't know about learning all the tackling techniques. One of the most important things to teach kids is tackling. But me not being a coach, I don't know how hard that is to teach.
>
> With that part aside, when it comes to the protocols there are certain things you look for. They really made it black and white. If they don't have it they don't have it, and if they do they do. If they have a headache or they're nauseated, then you take them out. Period."

She went on to confirm what I believe to be the greatest potential of harm to young players: "It's enough with the lines they've drawn. The question and biggest issue is if people always act on it." In Connie's opinion, time would be well spent in teaching what the potential side effects could be from an undiagnosed concussion, and the possible health risks associated with a player sent back into the game too quickly following a concussion.

She then discussed something that has changed her outlook on concussions: Secondary Impact Syndrome (SIS). SIS occurs when someone with a concussion receives another concussion prior to the previous one being completely healed.

After she watched a video about a young player who suffered a concussion, then minutes later was returned to the game where he received a secondary concussion that caused such horrific brain damage he became handicapped for the rest of his life, she said, "I saw that, and that is the line I'm not going to sit on."

Connie disclosed she's aware of two players at the high school who were permanently affected by concussions. Though one player had a primary or initial concussion where all protocol was followed, he developed brain bleeds following the concussion. Even though those typically heal, many of the other side effects due to a concussion don't.

She was also aware of a player who played at the University of Utah who in her words was "an amazing player." According to Connie:

> "He was doing great in football, gets a concussion but doesn't tell anyone about it and gets another one. He couldn't go to school, he couldn't practice, he couldn't play. We literally had to stick him in a dark room for three months straight.
>
> Every single day he'd come in the morning, we would sit him in a room and at the end of the night he would go home. I saw him referring a football game the other day and he is doing a lot better. But I think about what he could be doing."

At Riverton High School every football player is required to take what is called a Base Line Test every other year. This test establishes a baseline for each player individually on certain tasks of memory and reaction time like word skills, shapes, colors and numbers.

As the Certified Athletic Trainer, Connie is responsible to administer the tests as well as making sure each player is up-to-date on the test. She explains:

> "There are certain things that normally increase with concussions, one of them is reaction time which is usually .5 or .6 seconds.
>
> Usually with a concussion it will increase to .8 which is still under a second but is something to check. I've seen it as high as 1.5 seconds.
>
> The reason we have a base line is to see what their normal was, how did they react? What was their normal reaction time? Were they able to remember this? Were they able to remember four words normally or three or all five?
>
> With a concussion they are able to remember one word. Okay, it is pretty obvious that something is going on."

Once a normal baseline is established for each player, if a concussion is suspected the test would be readministered. Then the two tests would be compared by a qualified doctor to determine if a concussion may have occurred.

I shared with Connie that the Center for Disease Control (CDC) has reported that injuries in tackle football have increased 60% over the last decade. I asked her if during the years she's been working with football players if she's seen that type of an increase:

> "I honestly don't agree with that. I think the awareness has come up and not just concussions, but high ankle sprains where people used to just run on them, now we brace them up and tell them not to walk on it.
>
> I just think it is more awareness that has gone up and not actually the injuries themselves."

I asked her from a medical standpoint if there was a certain age she'd recommend youth could begin playing tackle football. Her answer was that she was less concerned with the age of the player than she was if the coach was going to teach proper techniques. She felt an 11-year-old would be more capable of following instructions if they were taught to keep their head up when tackling. So she concluded that 11 or 12 years old would be her personal recommendation to begin playing.

I shared with her that Tom Brady, quarterback for the New England Patriots and future Hall of Fame NFL player, reportedly wasn't allowed to play tackle football until he was 14. I also mentioned that some medical professionals believe a main danger associated with tackling prior to age 14 is the young person's body isn't proportionate to their head in order to offer enough support:

> "What I can see in research is it's not necessarily impact; it's the head whipping back that's causing more concussions than anything else. Yes, you have to wear your mouthpiece. And yes, you have to wear your helmet.
>
> When they get hit, their head gets flung back and their brain hits the back of their head. And then it flings forward and their brain hits the front of their head. It's the idea that little kids don't have enough strength to prevent that."

Our conversation concluded with a discussion surrounding being cleared to play football following a diagnosed or suspected concussion:

> "Just three ago while I was in college, in order to return to play the player would require light cardio that eventually led into drills for three or four days. Today it's five days minimum prior to returning to play.
>
> The first day they must go the entire day without any symptoms. The second day is a little bit of non-impact cardio like biking, swimming. Even that's not 100% -- it's more like 70%.

> The third day is light cardio impact, running or walking. The fourth day is actual drills and practice, and the fifth day is full contact, full practice and full game."

If any symptoms reoccur during any of the days, the workout is immediately suspended. The player is required to take a step back and return to it again the next day. Depending on where the player is during the five-day cycle, they may be required to return to day one in their recovery.

It's obvious from our interview that Connie is very supportive of the USA Heads Up Football program, and believes it goes a long way to increase awareness of the causes of concussions.

Her recommendation is that more time and effort be placed on informing parents and players about the possible risks involved in playing tackle football, including primary and secondary concussions.

CHAPTER SEVEN

CONDITIONING TO PREVENT INJURY

Football begins during the final hot days of summer, so attention needs to be paid to the heat element of the game. One of the contributing factors to injuries is that most programs begin the season with a rigorous conditioning camp.

The Utah High School Activity Association has implemented the "Heat-Acclimatization Period" as described below.

Football Heat Acclimatization Guidelines

Week 1:

July 22-26. No organized workouts; no pads; helmets only; conditioning and weightlifting only.

Week 2:

Official start date and team selection (approved March 13, 2013). July 29-August 3, helmets only (no other pads on players); football specific workouts (without equipment) are permissible. X's and O's and chalk talks are permitted.

Week 3:

Days 1 and 2 (August 5-6) helmets only (no other pads on players)! Football-specific workouts without equipment are permissible. X's and O's and chalk talks are permitted.

Days 3-5 (August 7-9) helmets and shoulder pads only! Contact with blocking sleds and tackling dummies may be initiated.

Day 6 (August 10) 100% live contact drills may begin.

"The heat-acclimatization period is defined as the initial 14 consecutive days of preseason practice for all student athletes. The goal of the acclimatization period is to enhance exercise heat tolerance and the ability to exercise safely and effectively in warm to hot conditions. This period should begin on the first day of practice or conditioning before the regular season."

Hydration

It's equally important to maintain proper hydration before, during, and after practice and games. In order to properly hydrate for an event like practice, workout, or a game, a player must begin the hydration process at least a half hour prior to the event. USA Football liaison, Dave Csillan, has recommended the following guidelines for proper hydration:

How much should you drink before and after activity?
Drink 12 fluid ounces 30 minutes before activity begins. After activity, drink every 20 minutes during the first hour to make up for fluid loss.

What should you drink?
Cold water is the best fluid to drink during activity and allows for fast absorption. It's a myth that cold water gives stomach cramps. Sports drinks work well after activity to help replenish lost electrolytes.

How much should you drink during exercise?
Children under 90 pounds should drink 5 ounces every 20 minutes, and children more than 90 pounds should drink 9 ounces every 20 minutes.

Easy tip: A child's gulp equals half an ounce of fluid. Therefore, a child 90 pounds or less should drink at least 10 gulps every 20 minutes.

What is the thirst response?
Don't allow thirst to be your guide to drinking. By the time you feel thirsty, you are already dehydrated.

What color should your urine be?
Your urine should look like lemonade and not apple juice. Urine color can be a non-scientific indicator that the body is becoming, or already is, dehydrated.

Larry Kenney, PhD, professor of physiology and kinesiology at Penn State, stated the following regarding hydration in sports:

> "Very slight changes in body water may create some performance issues in sports; as little as a 2% decrease in body water can lead to dehydration and performance detriments in sports. When your water levels decrease by higher levels like 3% or 4%, there are physiological changes that occur that may have health consequences, such as increased heart rate and body temperature."

It's highly recommended that coaching staffs provide and implement a hydration plan, including providing fluids for coaches and athletes during and prior to events. Most people don't realize that there are many foods that contain water and can be used to hydrate the body.

During every halftime, our coaching staff at Riverton High School provides the athletes and coaches sliced oranges that contain 90% water, and are a great source for fluids to hydrate the body.

CHAPTER EIGHT

THE MENTAL AND EMOTIONAL PITFALLS OF FOOTBALL

As previously mentioned, much attention has been paid to the physical aspect of football. Unfortunately, the same attention hasn't been given to the harm caused by the ınd emotional pitfalls and challenges of the game.

There are news reports about players, coaches and/or parents in most sports abusing young players, or abusing the officials in front of the players. For example, you may have read about a catastrophic event surrounding a soccer official who was refereeing a game in Taylorsville, Utah.

On April 27, 2014, Portillo called a foul on a 17-year-old player that resulted in a yellow card (a warning). Upset over the call, Jose Domingo Teran angrily punched Portillo in the side of the head.

Experiencing dizziness and vomiting blood, Ricardo was taken to the hospital with what initially appeared to be a minor injury, but slipped into a coma and later passed away.

His daughter, Johana, said her father's passion was soccer. "'People don't know it's a game. We're all there to have fun, not to go and kill each other." His daughters had begged him to stop refereeing, but he refused to quit as he loved soccer.

This wasn't the first time the referee had suffered an injury at the hands of an angry player during his eight years in the recreational league. Five years prior a player upset with a call broke his ribs. A few years before that a player broke his leg.

As Teran pleaded guilty to homicide by assault as part of a plea deal, he stated to the judge that "I was frustrated at the ref and caused his death." Ricardo Portillo was only 46 years old when a single temperamental punch in the head took his life.

Fighting Isn't Limited Just to Players

Though physical violence outside the rules of the sport is completely unacceptable, there seems to be a tolerance of acceptance in far too many cases.

If you've watched or participated in ice hockey, you've probably witnessed numerous fights between players. (I'll admit I often "go to a fight hoping an ice hockey game will break out.")

I'm constantly amazed when the referees stand back and allow the fight to happen. Allowing such actions to occur without any consequences to the players or teams sends a very poor message to the participants as well as the spectators.

Most of the time a fight or punches in football results in a 15-yard penalty. However, in ice hockey it seems like a debacle is celebrated.

Having coached multiple sports for a number of years, I've seen a lot of violent acts such as officials being knocked out by a parent's punch, or an official suffering a broken shoulder after they were tackled by a teen player.

I've also witnessed many coaches and parents being ejected from all sorts of sporting events for unruly, out-of-control behavior.

While participating in a baseball tournament I had to stop one of my assistant coaches who angrily had his son (a player on the team) pinned against a cement wall in the dugout and was yelling at him (again -- *his son!*). I've also witnessed a coach throw a baseball at one of the players that caused an injury to their leg.

During a basketball game I witnessed the coach for the other team become so upset at the officials that he pulled a "Bobby Knight tantrum" by throwing his chair onto the court.

While attending a girls' basketball tournament in Las Vegas, I got caught in the middle of two fathers from opposing teams in a full-blown fist fight.

In many cases physical harm will heal in a short period of time, but emotional harm can last for years if not forever. All kinds of abuse exist in sports and far too often it is tolerated for many reasons, none of which are sufficient to justify the action or tolerance of the action.

CHAPTER NINE

INTERVIEW WITH MATT WELLS HEAD COACH UTAH STATE UNIVERSITY

The initial inspiration for this book came in the spring of 2014 during a coaching clinic in Wendover, Nevada, where the keynote speaker was Coach Matt Wells, the head football coach at Utah State University. As he spoke I was bowled over by his passion for the game of football as well as compassion for his players.

He said that one of his mentoring methods was to demand accountability from them relating to their lives socially, academically and athletically on and off the field. And to teach them that improper behavior in any of those three areas will have a negative effect on the team which consequently produces a negative result on the field. He said, "If they are under achieving in the classroom they will under achieve on the field."

During his speech Coach Wells commented on news reports portraying tackle football as unsafe. When he said, "Is tackle football safe? Of course it is," for the first time I reflected on the question that ultimately caused me to reanalyze my position about players' safety on and off the field.

Because his statement deeply resonated with me, I decided to write this book about the short and long-term ramifications of injuries due to the lack of proper equipment, training and education in youth tackle football.

Wells, a former Aggie quarterback, began coaching over 18 years ago, the year following his graduation from Utah State University. During his career as a student athlete at USU, he was a player on two conference championship teams. His initial coaching experience came when he joined the Naval Academy football staff. After five years he moved on to the University of Tulsa where he remained for five more years.

Coach Wells then found a home with the New Mexico coaching staff. After two years there he spent nine months at the University of Louisville, then went back to New Mexico for an additional year.

In 2011, Wells returned to his alma mater (USU) as the offensive coordinator and quarterbacks coach. After two years as an assistant coach he was promoted to head coach where he led his team to a seven-and-one conference record, which positioned them to play in the inaugural Big West Conference championship game.

After leading the Aggies to their third-ever bowl victory Wells was named the 2013 Mountain West Coach of the Year. The Aggies finished the season with nine wins and only five losses.

> "I think youth football is awesome for many reasons: It teaches young kids a team sport, a team concept. In my opinion I think football is the greatest team sport ever invented.
>
> You can't do it as an individual. It teaches early stages of teaching kids selflessness. Another positive is that it's an active sport. Kids are out of the house off iPads, off phones and off videogames."

I asked him if he felt the equipment his program uses is sufficient:

> "It's getting better and better every year. There's continually the technology and improvements. The first thing you think of are the helmets, and the way they have revolutionized the helmets these days is unbelievable to me.
>
> The second thing from the college level that continues to improve is the coaches, trainers, and the doctors and the administrators are all more on the same page. And practice times, practice amounts and the physicalness in the practice are limited.
>
> The acclimatization periods at the very beginning we all have to go through -- whether it's spring practice or training camp -- the limitation is on two-a-days and on full tackling. I think that's all positive.
>
> The programs I've been in the last ten years have already moved towards that without the NCAA coming down. So I felt like we were already on track for that on a player's health standpoint. I think at this level those steps have already been taken, and I think that's a very positive thing.

> Equipment-wise, I do think it's better. Obviously the biggest thing right now are concussions and head injuries. The NCAA and the coaches have looked at it, and from our standpoint it's been those limitations on training camp and practice restrictions. Then as well the targeting penalty that's now enforced and different techniques involved.
>
> I think that's progressive, so I would think that's mirrored in the lower levels. If that's the case, I think that's a positive for the sport."

***"Our best coaches are coaching our best players, and that's in the professional football. Our worst coaches are coaching the most critical position,
and that is the 9, 10, 11-year-old people."***
~Chris Carter

In response to my question of what age is appropriate for a young boy or girl to start tackle football, Coach Wells answered:

> "I think it's reflective of two things: Number one, is the kid's body and his makeup relative to the other kids at that age he's going to be playing with and against? That's the first thing. Because if you put the number at seven, and he's a smaller kid, they're all small right?
>
> [Maybe he's an] underdeveloped kid, or he's maybe not mentally ready yet, or maybe he's not really into outdoor sports yet, or maybe he needs another year or two. I don't know that answer, but I think it's relative to the one individual kid.
>
> Then I think it's directly relative to the second thing, which I think is the most important: Are they going to get taught to tackle and block correctly? End of story. Then I think it's safe, it's healthy and they'll have fun.

> But my concern is how they're getting taught to tackle and to block. Not catch, not throw, nor run. Every kid runs, throws and catches the ball on the playground -- some better than others.
>
> But you don't block on the playground. You don't just wake up tackling. Now that's not all true, because I think some kids come out of the womb tackling and running into everything."

During our conversation I came to the conclusion that he believes proper teaching requires better educated coaches:

> "I think coaches at any level can be trained, me included, pro guys included. We all do professional development. We all go and learn new techniques. We get confirmed on the technique or the drills or the schemes we're using.
>
> Our medical and our equipment staffs use the off-season to go explore other ideas, to go confirm things they've been doing. We all do that, and I think every level should do that.
>
> I think it needs to be the individual coach's responsibility at every level to seek new ways and new research and confirm what you're doing. I think it's being humble and understanding you can always improve, and what are you in it for in the first place? Why am I in college football right now? If it's not for the kids, I'm in it for the wrong reason."

Our discussion then turned to preparing and assisting athletes to move to the next level -- an area I believe many coaches have lost sight of:

> "I think it's our job as mentors or coaches to do that. But it's very much human nature to lose sight of that quite often. I think it's our job to come back to a baseline of why I'm this to begin with, and what's my ultimate goal?

> I understand that for me at this level I'll be evaluated on wins and losses, and I'll get evaluated on whether my kids graduate or not. But sometimes we get so caught up in a win or a loss that we forget we're molding that kid for life.
>
> Which to me is the next level, because only 1.5% of these kids are going to the League, although we're seeking that ultimate prize, that ultimate goal of a Bowl game championship. That's my level, but I think everybody that understands why you're really in it will continue to go back to that baseline."

Coach Wells' comment about the rest of the players' lives being the next level truly enlightened me. Having coached with Coach Miller for years (please see his interview in this book as well), I now realize that placing a focus on preparing athletes for life should be status quo for coaches. It's not only about preparing them for the next level in the sport, but also their next level in life.

The Centers for Disease Control (CDC) says that injuries have gone up 60% in tackle football over the last decade. Coach Wells said he hasn't witnessed that kind of increase during his career:

> "I don't know where that [number] is coming from. Sixty percent is quite staggering. There's no question that in 18 years I haven't seen that in colleges. That's very surprising to me that it would be that high."

I was pleased to learn he'd heard of the USA Football's Heads Up program the NFL has been involved in. When I asked him what he thought about implementing it into the youth football program he replied...

> "I will concur that it's a step in the right direction. But I think with anything in life, as they say 'time is money.' The more time you spend, the better we're all going to be. So I think the more time someone spends learning, researching, visiting professional development, somebody will be better trained and more knowledgeable."

There are many people advocating that kids play flag football until they reach high school where they can be taught proper tackling techniques. I asked Coach Wells what effect he thought that would have on his program and higher up in the NFL:

> "I don't know about that. I think kids can get taught how to properly tackle while they're in middle school and junior high. I wonder if that would be put into place if it wouldn't derail a kid's excitement and passion for the game, and move them into other things or other sports, which wouldn't be bad.
>
> But I'm not sure how that would be helping the game of football from an interest level. If you're a golfer you can only hit off the tee until you're in high school. You can't go putt and chip. If you're a basketball player, you can't shoot a three-pointer until you're in high school. In football you can't tackle.
>
> So that would be my question: If they're properly taught, and they're physically able to do it at a middle school/junior high level, then I think it's a positive for football and the direction that we have been going and should continue to go."

Already extremely impressed with Matt, during our interview I gained even more respect for him as a coach and mentor to his players and coaches. Especially when he talked about attending coaching clinics during the off-season and receiving confirmation of why he coaches.

He has more than 100 players plus coaches on his team he's ultimately responsible for –a daunting responsibility he's comfortable with and excels at.

It's obvious his passion is the team and players, and everything he does is with them in mind. A sure sign of a great coach.

Wanting to be on the side of blitzing or going down the field one too many times, he also subscribes to the school of erring on the side of aggressiveness. In the chapter "Coaches and Coaching" I shared our local basketball coaches opposite school of thought, "tail firmly placed between the legs" strategy. Wells expressed how important it is as a coach to determine your expectations, teach it to the team, and then demand it from them.

He understands that although all players work together as a team, they are individuals and therefore have to be treated as such. He also made it clear the expectations and rules are the same for everyone, but the interactions related to each player have to be different.

I'd like to extend a special thanks to Coach Wells for taking time to meet with me. I've been blessed by the experience, and am convinced he and his team will have great success.

CHAPTER TEN

INTERVIEW WITH MIKE MILLER FORMER HEAD COACH RIVERTON HIGH SCHOOL

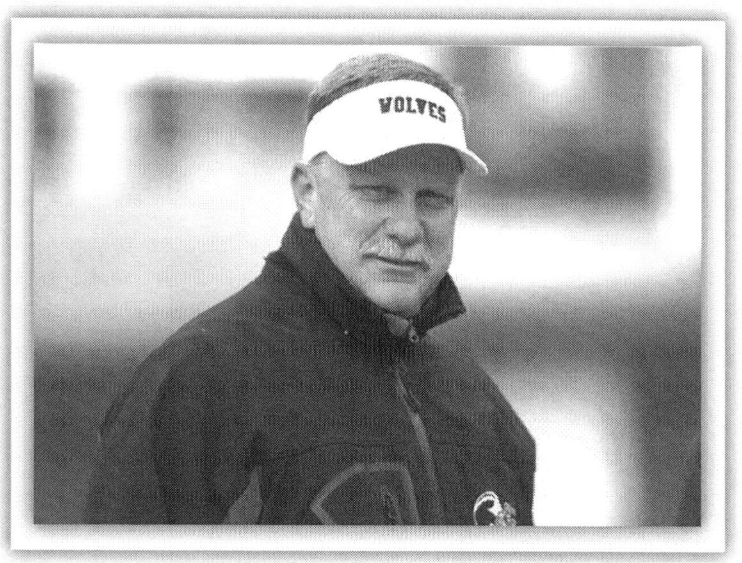

In January of 2015, Coach Mike Miller stepped down from his stellar 29-year career as a high school football to start over in school administration.

Mike is much more than just a football coach and teacher as he's also a father figure and mentor to many people. His passion is unparalleled because he demands the same focus, dedication and team spirit from his all his players and coaches.

In 2010 I was coaching my son's Little League team. Not having much experience as a coordinator, I observed the high school's practices to learn what I needed to be coaching defense.

Mike had an open door policy for any youth coaches in Riverton, Utah, as he allowed us to copy his playbook as well as watching many training and coaching DVDs from his library. Without fail he'd always approach me when I attended his practices to discuss how things were going.

During the spring of 2011, Mike asked my daughter (one of his classroom aids) if I was going to be coaching Little League football that fall. At the time I was working toward a position coaching high school basketball for a school outside our area, so she told him she didn't think that was in my plans.

Shortly thereafter I received a call from him to discuss taking a position as coach on his staff. After reviewing this with my business partner and my wife, I concluded I wouldn't be able to commit to the time required. However, by the fall of 2012, because my business demands had changed I was finally free to accept his kind offer.

Although I had *coached* Little League football for a few years prior to 2010, I knew very little about *teaching* high school football. It was exciting to watch experienced coaches instructing the team in every aspect of the game including the position of the arms, head, eyes, feet and legs.

I also had the stark realization how little I really knew to effectively coach Little League teams.

About Coach Miller

Coach Miller played football at Kearns High School in Utah, and from there he played at Dixie College in St. George. Following his stint as a student athlete, he was invited to help one of his buddies coach a ninth grade Little League team.

There were five coaches when the season began, but by the end of the year it was just him and his buddy who only had time to coach every other week, which left Mike holding down the fort the rest of the time.

The following year he asked the new head coach at Kearns High School if he could coach the ninth grade sophomore team, then was moved up to coaching the linebackers on the varsity team where he also helped with the offensive line.

After three years Mike was promoted to the position of defensive coordinator where he remained for an additional three years.

His experiences at Kearns convinced him to change his career direction from becoming a physical therapist to a high school teacher and football coach. Subsequent to coaching stops at Woods Cross and Brighton High Schools, he ended up at Olympus High as the defensive coordinator.

After four years he was promoted to head coach for the first time in his career.

After five years at Olympus he was offered the head coaching job at Riverton High where he remained until he retired from coaching.

Mike's Thoughts on Youth Tackle Football

During my interview with Mike, I asked him to share his opinion on today's youth tackle football (which includes Little League as well as high school), and if he felt improvements should be made to the equipment:

"I didn't start playing football until I was in the sixth grade, but had a bunch of friends who were playing before that.

My experiences were good. Back then the equipment wasn't anything like it is today, but today it's vastly improved.

I think research has shown that if you take a group of eight-year-olds and have them play football, if you have a team of twenty-five I think only six to eight of them end up playing high school football. So I'm not quite sure it's good to get them started that early.

I think around junior high and middle school age is a good time for kids to start. At that point they don't bump their head quite as much, and the equipment is better as they get older because helmet companies make a better helmet for bigger heads.
As a young man I think I got more concussions probably playing sandlot football than wearing protective gear. When I and my buddies would go out and play tackle football without any football equipment on, we'd get kneed in the head or our heads would hit the hard ground. So I probably saw more stars doing that than I ever did playing football.

But I think it's something that has to be looked at and addressed. I think the good thing about youth tackle football is if it's taught properly (which is a whole other issue) the equipment prevents [bad] things from occurring.

I think a couple things in society have changed to make us more aware of it. For instance, they've taken all that roughhousing and that kind of playing off the playgrounds at schools. So for a kid to bump his head or something like that, it's saving the kid a little bit. But it makes him a little more concerned when something does happen, which is probably good.

I'll give you an example: I had a kid in football hit his funny bone, and he thought his arm was going to fall off. He came up me concerned he was going to be paralyzed. Three minutes later the burning sensation went away and he was fine.

Today's kids can get the same thrill of running and tackling by playing a videogame where there are no injuries and no fitness involved. Whereas we used to have to run around and get the thrill after watching Saturday and Sunday football games. All week long we pretended to be those athletes, and then got bumped up a little bit.

I think the big concern with Little League football is the equipment maintenance. Some people do a great job – some don't. I've seen some just gather it and throw it into storage units, then pulled out the next year.

I've also seen people go through them and have it looked at and reconditioned. There are reconditioning companies that NOCSAE-approve [National Operating Committee on Standards for Athletic Equipment] every helmet. They'll do shoulder pads and everything else, so I think it's good if it's reconditioned.

The other concern I have with Little League football is the coaching aspect. I don't know if coaches buy a couple videos and then do what's on those videos. A lot of times Little League coaches don't have to be concerned with football until a week or two before tryouts where someone at my level, or even greater levels, were researching it all year. My experience has been they pull it out a week before the season starts and suit up the kids.

The ironic thing with Little League in our area is kids get their pads, and after three days of tryouts they put them on and start hitting and hit for weeks. But as a high school team, I can't do that for two weeks.

For example, we have our one-a-days for one week, and then the next week is a game week. To me, it seems like Little League hit for three weeks before they even get into a week of game preparation.

> As a parent of a Little League kid, one of my concerns would be all the hitting they do prior to their first game. I think there should be some regulations on how many weeks they have to go before they put on the pads and start hitting."

I told Mike that in his book, *Head Game: Football's Concussion Crises*, Chris Nowinski said, "The average child will be hit in the head 1 to 300 times. Many youth programs don't have any medical personnel on the sideline, which means that most concussions won't be identified. Children have biomechanical disadvantages that come from having a giant head on a small body, and that the developing brain is more sensitive to trauma":

> "I think once they hit junior high or middle school age they start into puberty, so I think at that point it's not bad for them to play. In a perfect world they'd be fully developed by the time they'd start playing, but I don't think that's going to happen. I think they have to start developing at a young age, because the expectations put on these kids by their parents and other people to go to the next level, as they say.
>
> I often laugh because we have parents who have expectations for us to help their kids develop to the point where they can get a Division I scholarship. But when you compare us to Texas and Florida, and the way they run their programs and the compensation for the off season stuff, they're at an advantage in terms of that.
>
> On the other hand, I think this state [Utah] does a great job monitoring and regulating the high school and up. We have all kinds of stipulations we have to follow as we go through camps that have changed that.
>
> The cool thing about little kids is they're kind of rubbery and can bounce. They're not as brittle as older players as they can hurt their arm and it heals fine. The problem is it's less forgiving since their brains are just developing. But nowadays if kids are given the proper equipment, I think they're more protected than when they're trying to play without it."

I told him the CDC made a statement that "in the last decade injuries from tackle football have increased 60%":

> "I haven't witnessed that in my program. To differentiate between discomfort and injury, I've actually seen a decline in injuries. I've seen more kids that will be concerned – and trainers will have to look at things – more than in the old days where a kid could scuff up something and he'd keep going because he knew what discomfort felt like with any little pain.
>
> But I think injuries have actually decreased, and I think a lot of rules have helped that. In fact, I recently read that percentage-wise, according to the population that plays, there are more injuries in soccer and basketball than in football.
>
> Statistically you can look at it any way you want. I have 135 football players. Our basketball coach will probably have 30 kids in his whole program. If three kids in his program turn their ankle that's 10% of his team, whereas for me to get 10% I've got to have 13 or 14.
>
> I think football is a barbaric sport. There are going to be some pains and discomforts. But for the most part to me it seems the major injuries have decreased, and I think a lot of that has to do with the equipment and the rules."

When Mike was asked if he was aware of the Heads Up Football standard USA Football launched that includes the Player Safety Coach pilot program that promotes a better, safer game on youth levels (plus, the training course the CDC implemented):

> "It's designed to train coaches as well as League administrators in proper tackling technique and concussion recognition. To become a certified administrator or coach for this you have to go through a training that lasts about an hour-and-a-half."

I then asked him if he thought an hour-and-a-half was long enough to be adequately trained on how to recognize a concussion, and train and teach proper tackling and blocking techniques:

> "If you've been doing it properly, an hour-and-a-half's probably sufficient. If you've never done it before, you can spend over an hour to an hour-and-a-half and not even get to tip of the iceberg in terms of tackling.
>
> I think tackling is very important. I've always taught my kids to bring their chest to the man and club up. I gave them a target's name and points. But for the most part we just try to chest to the man, club up and wrap up, and bring your feet to him.
>
> I think people learning how to teach tackling isn't as important as using some logic when they're tackling. I've seen two ten-year-old Little League guys ten yards apart, and have them run straight at each other. The truth is when you tackle, very few times it's nose-to-nose head on. If you're going to do anything fast and full speed, you ought to be close and you ought to give angles so you can take on the blow a little more with the shoulder. I've seen guys line up kids and run right at each other and hit each other.
>
> A lot of times I've found that concussions don't occur by the front-on contact. What I've found is that concussions usually occur from side hits on the side or back of the head. In my career I've had more kids experience concussion problems when someone runs by and their knee hits them in the ear or in the back of their head.
>
> For me, if you can keep your chin and your head up -- and actually have a target or a place where you're going to place your head to take the blow on with a shoulder -- I think that helps prevent concussions more than just running at each other, ducking your head, and trying to hit with the crown of your head.

I think if you keep your chin up, put your face on a target, slide and take on the blow with your shoulder, I think you're much better off.

A lot of people do tackle drills their coach did with them, or ones they might have seen on the Internet. I think they ought to be more educated about the proper way to tackle than be creative to think of drills that aren't high impact with tackling. We tackle from our knees, and we'll do that in some of those kind of things as well."

Mike answered a definitive "Yes" when asked if he thought Little Leagues should require coaches to have more training in those areas before they let them coach:

"I hope you put this in a way that I'm not dogging on any Little League program. But it's been my experience that those guys are busy with other aspects of their life, so their motivation might be their son's on the team or something like that.
They just jump into it a week or two before it starts, and then they hurry and speed them through some so-called training to get them certified so they can coach because they may not have enough coaches.

I think there should be requirements early in the year where all of them – even the old guys like me – should have to learn and revisit tackling training before they can coach. But I know Little Leagues are sometimes in a position where they're limited to who can and who can't coach."

We discussed Sean Pamphilon's documentary, *The United States of Football* (I mention this in several places throughout my book as it's a very powerful testimony to long-term effects of head injuries), where Chris Carter said, "Our best coaches are coaching our best players, and that's in the professional football. Our worst coaches are coaching the most critical position, and that is the 9, 10, 11-year-old people.":

> "Well, I'm not sure the best coaches are in the NFL because I don't know if they have to do a whole lot of coaching. They do a lot of scheming and looking for matchups, and just trying to keep the players in shape.
>
> The techniques they teach in the NFL are far different than the techniques you'd teach in ninth, tenth and eleventh grades, so I wouldn't totally agree with Chris Carter. I've seen some great Little League coaches – I really have – the guys who educate themselves and take it real personal.
>
> The difference between an NFL guy and a Little League guy is this: My dad, brother and built our cabin, finished our basement, and we've done all this construction work together. But we don't do it all the time, so I wouldn't consider me being an expert at building homes.
>
> If you take a guy who builds homes all day, and he's going to coach football, he's going to put in a little bit of time to get ready for football like I would to build a home. During that time you're going to be extremely committed to doing it. But when it's done you hang up the tool belt, move forward with your life, and focus on things that take care of your family. Whereas when you're a football coach by profession, that's what your focus is year-round.
>
> So just because I've built a few homes and have done some construction, I'm not as good as the guy who does it every day although I can do it. It's the same with the guy who coaches football all the time. I consider him a little more of an expert by definition because he does it all the time. But that doesn't necessarily mean he's a better coach, because I think great coaches are great teachers who take it very personally."

Mike mentioned that sixth and seventh grade is probably a good age to start playing tackle football. But I was curious to know if they waited until high school, and were playing flag football until then, what effect he thought that could have on high school and college programs:

"I don't think that's a bad idea. Again, I don't want this to sound like I'm dogging on any Little League programs. But first of all, a lot of kids who get to play and their dad's the coach, when they get to high school they usually quit because they're not pampered through the program like they were when their dad was the coach.

As hard as it is to be a father at home and a coach on the field, they're still fathers on the field. I don't blame them – I love my son just as much. It probably would be even a little harder because my expectations would be even greater for him.

Letting them start in the ninth grade actually wouldn't be a bad thing. But it's twofold: 1) I have a lot of kids who have bad experiences through Little League and never want to play; or 2) pick up really bad habits while they're in Little League because their coach is more of a schemes guy, or an X's and O's guy rather than a fundamentals guy.

So I fight three years of trying to break some bad habits they develop in Little League.

Sometimes when we get a young man who's never played, he's probably not as productive as a sophomore. But every year I have kids in their senior year who only started playing as a sophomore who are big impact guys.

I don't think it's a bad thing if they've had a good experience and are well-coached, and they build some confidence in Little League. But it's twofold: I think with the good there's the bad that develop with some of them.

I struggle because there are parents whose kids have played all through Little League. They tell you how great they are, and that they should be a college athlete and all those kinds of things. But when they're in the ninth grade there are a lot of things that have to occur developmentally by the time they get into high school.

Little League gives the smaller kid a chance to experience football, and that's a plus. For example, when I was in ninth grade I only weighed 128 pounds. I think I entered high school at 136 pounds and 5'4" to 5'6", and I obviously grew to be a lot bigger man.

But it was the experiences and the best Little League coaches ever like Stan Carsey in sixth and seventh grade, and then Al Sprouse in eighth and ninth grade who might have been the best coaches I ever had (which includes high school and college). My head coach in high school, Bruce Takeno, was also a phenomenal coach.

So there are some good and some bad. If they didn't let kids play until they were in ninth grade, I'd probably be very supportive of that. Out of all of my senior class most had started when they were eight and nine years old. I didn't start until sixth grade, and there were only two of us that went and played college football – me and another guy who started about the same time I did.

> A lot of times the big problem is with the real little guys (you'll hear this all the time). Dad will take him in to get his equipment, and the dad's more excited about his little eight-year old playing football than the eight-year-old is.
>
> I even had
> one dad say, "We've been waiting for this forever," but the little kid wasn't even paying attention. So I think it would be wise to start it a little later."

A word of advice Mike would like to give parents of Little Leaguers...

> "The things I always tell people when they come and talk to me is to do a little research and find out about the coach and their age group. I'd see what his background is and what his experiences have been, more than just winning and losing.
>
> For me the kid should be enjoying the experience and learning good, basic fundamentals. So I think the wins and losses will take care of themselves.
>
> What happens is we get Little League coaches with bigger playbooks than I have because they've read it in the book or have seen some things. They keep trying to get these kids to run 100 plays when in reality no one can do that. Not even the NFL guys do it.
>
> So I always tell them to do a background check to see how it is. If it's not working out for you, maybe just stay with flag football a little bit to learn the finesse part of the game.
>
> But if you do a little research, and it seems like the coach is a good coach who has the kid's best interest at heart, just let the kid have a great experience and have fun playing so he decides that he enjoys the game and continues playing it even when it gets a little rougher on his body."

...and then to Little League coaches:

"The same thing I just told you about the parents. I've talked to Little League coaches about adhering to the basic fundamentals. I've talked to them about letting the kids have a great experience, build up their confidence a little bit and let them have some fun. But again, to adhere to good old basic fundamentals.

Then as soon as the meeting breaks they're all drawing X's and O's on the board, and concerned about winning more than developing. I think they need to worry about developing these young kids properly, which is far more important than winning.

When you're not succeeding – but you're trying to develop these young men into functional people in society – it's harder to get them to do what you're trying to get them to do off the field to be good people.

When you're winning it's easier to get them to do those things off the field that makes them great people more than great football players.

Winning also helps make it easier around the house on the weekends for my family because I don't pout as much. So that's why winning is important to me.

I think there's too much importance placed on winning, which is why coaches try to get every kid they can to come to their school. But I'm just the opposite.

When a kid comes to me, they've got to be classy or I won't let them in my program. I keep track of how many wins and losses I have in a year, but I don't know if that's the most important thing about winning."

Of course, it's difficult to capture the greatness of a veteran coach like Mike Miller during a brief half-hour interview.

I never attended a post-game meeting where he didn't tell the team how much he loved them and they knew he meant it. Even when he was angry and frustrated that they suffered a loss, the players still knew how much he cared about them.

He made sure everyone knew the game was never about him and his assistant coaches, which is the sign of a great coach. To Mike the game is always about the young men and women trainers in his program, and preparing his players to be successful in life after high school and college.

CHAPTER ELEVEN

INTERVIEW WITH JOHN MADSEN UNIVERSITY OF UTAH RECEIVER AND NFL TIGHT END

John Madsen, former NFL player for the Oakland Raiders and Cleveland Browns, currently owns and operates his Salt Lake-based company John Madsen Performance (JMP) where he trains youth of all ages, from those just beginning their sporting career to those preparing to enter college and professional athletics. With a great passion for helping athletes achieve their goals and dreams, John helps many young college football players prepare for the NFL combine, a week-long showcase every February at Lucas Oil Stadium in Indianapolis, where they perform physical and mental tests in front of coaches, general managers, and scouts.

Even though John started playing tackle football when he was of nine years old, when he reached tenth grade he realized he was too small for the sport, and turned to playing high school baseball and basketball (albeit his basketball team didn't win many games).

When he began attending Snow College in Utah, he felt his athletic ability was sufficient to secure him a spot on one of the teams. At the same time he was waiting for basketball tryouts, football tryouts were beginning. He decided that rather than betting it all on basketball, he'd try out for football and leave basketball as a backup. It was an exciting day for John Madsen when he learned he'd made the football team.

He played for Snow College for one season. During the off-season he thought long and hard about his career. Without an appointment he requested a meeting with Urban Meyer, the head football coach at the University of Utah, or someone from his staff:

> "I remember reading this article and thinking that I just want to go up and talk to them. So I drove home from Snow College one weekend, and went up there on a Friday. I didn't Have an appointment – I just walked in the building and asked for a wide receiver or head coach.
>
> The coach was in a staff meeting. The GA I met poked his head in and said, 'Hey, I've got about a 6'5" wide receiver who wants to talk to somebody.' So Urban and Billy Gonzales, a wide receiver coach, comes walking out of the meeting. They looked at me and told me to come with them. They sat me down in a chair and just started grilling me with quick questions. I didn't even have time to think. They were like, 'Who are you? What's your background? What are you doing here?'"

Three weeks later John was officially enrolled at the University of Utah. Instantly becoming a member of Coach Meyer's football team, it didn't take long for him to see playing time.

The second game of his first season the Utes were playing at Texas A&M in front of 100,000 fans. Just prior to the end of the first half the Utes were losing 28 to 0 when their starting receiver broke his ribs and was done for the game. John quickly found himself on the playing field:

> "I was out there running around like crazy. I ended up making two big catches in the fourth quarter: One was a 30-yard fourth-and-15 catch. I jumped over the top of somebody and caught it.
>
> And then with eight seconds to go, we had climbed all the way the back. It was 28 to 20, and we were lined up on our own 40-yardline. We had one play left, and I just ran straight down the field. The quarterback threw the ball up. I found myself open in the end zone and caught the ball. So I ended the game with two catches for 93 yards and a touchdown. We ended up losing 28 to 26."

Urban Meyers obviously experienced a great deal of success with his teams. Discussing what John liked or disliked about him, and what kind of a coach he was...

> "I think he's going to go down in history as one of the best football coaches ever. What sets him apart from any coach I've ever had is obviously he's a smart football coach. He knows X's and O's. He understands offense and defense and special teams, and everything about football.
>
> But I think two things really sets him apart: Number one is his own mindset and the type of leader he is, so that every person in the room – whether it's a trainer, every player on the team, every coach on the coaching staff -- and everybody in that building believes that no matter who we're going to play we can win. I've never been part of a team or program that was built like that. He does it everywhere. He has a belief that he instills in most importantly the players.

> But it's also the coaching staff, the trainers and everybody in the room. I can't explain how everybody truly believed that no matter who we we're going to play (i.e., an SEC team – we ran the Mountain West back then when we were 6:0 against Pac-10 teams) we thought we were going to win. So being part of that was awesome, and I think that's what sets him apart."

We see athletes on the field playing with great talent and think they have it made. John shared with me during the interview how he had tried to quit:

> "My first year before I got to Texas A&M, a lot of people don't know this but I tried to quit. I was about two weeks into a training camp, and thought I had some broken ribs as I could barely breathe.
>
> I had a really rough scrimmage, and was just getting the crap beat out of me. I'd never experienced something so hard in my life.
>
> I made the decision that I was going to tell them thanks for the opportunity. But I really didn't love football. I was in over my head, and that was going to be my career. I had my bags packed in the dorms, and I was set on quitting.
>
> Before I could tell him, the crazy thing was he looked at me in the team meeting he always conducted and asked me if I was all right, and I said 'Yes.' He said, 'No, you're not. Go to my office.' He had one of the other coaches do the team meeting that night.
>
> When I got up to his office I said, 'Coach, I appreciate the opportunity, but I don't think I love football. I really appreciate you giving me the chance to play.' I remember those words vividly as that's exactly how I said them. By that time I was choking back tears.

> I didn't want to quit, but I didn't know what else to do because I'd never experienced something that hard. He looked at me and said, 'If you walk out those doors I'll find you.
>
> I've coached football for 18 years, and I've never seen raw talent like you have. I won't let you quit.' So he sat me down in the chair and wouldn't let me quit, and that made all the difference."

The sign of a great coach is they care about every player. If I knew nothing more about Coach Urban Meyer, I'd conclude that he's a great coach based on that alone. The fact he'd leave a team meeting to have a personal conversation with one of his players is amazing to me.

Our conversation then turned to injuries John experienced during his career as an athlete, such as when he broke his leg his senior year at the University of Utah:

> "I had a concussion my junior year. I think I probably had more than one concussions, but that was the one time when I kind of lost consciousness for a second. Everything went dark, and I didn't know where the heck I was.
>
> As far as other things that really took me out, there were multiple thing like spraining knees, AC joint shoulder (I separated a shoulder one time), broken fingers. A hip pointer was very painful, and was actually what ended me in Cleveland. I couldn't practice for two weeks at that training camp. And once you're in the training room your fate is kind of sealed.
>
> I was playing at San Diego State. I was coming in motion from the outside-in, and came across the quarterback. My job was to cut the defensive end, so I just kind of dove at him.

A big 270-pound guy put his knee right into my helmet, and the next thing I knew the training staff and Urban were looking over me. Everybody was there asking what happened.

It's weird, because I remember certain things in the moment. I remember saying, 'I don't know. Everything just went black,' so they were really worried. They were going to put me on a stretcher because that was kind of protocol, but not as much as it is now as I had a say back then.

The first thing I thought of was my mom and dad in the stands. *If I get on a stretcher and get wheeled out of here, my mom will be running on this field guaranteed.* I said, 'No, I'm fine. I'm going to walk off this field,' so I got helped off into the sideline.

Then I remember the doctors telling me they were going to give me three random words that I had to remember. The one I still remember was 'red dog.' It didn't mean anything, but I remember the trainer saying it. Then there were two other ones and I kept repeating them over and over to myself because I wanted to remember and go back into the game.

The trainer came back and started talking to me about something else. And then asked me what one of the words was and I couldn't remember. Going into the locker room after that I didn't know exactly where my locker and stuff were.

The concussion was different than I'd ever had because I had a headache for quite a while. I'd forget little things. For example, I played on Saturday, and then the following Wednesday my family had a birthday party at restaurant at Trolley Square. I grew up in Salt Lake City and had been there a million times. I was driving around and had to call my mom because I didn't know where Trolley Square was. So little things like that were weird because that wasn't normal for me.

> Then I played against Colorado State that next week. I remember making dumb mistakes that really wasn't like me. A couple times I lined up on the wrong side of the ball, or just really weird things because my mind wasn't functioning it normally would. When the lights go out for a second it's a scary experience."

John was asked several questions before sending him back into the game the next week, such as if he was sensitive to light or had a headache. Then while he was on an exercise bike they asked if he felt light-headed:

> "I don't know if I had any of those symptoms Thursday and Friday. I know I didn't practice all week until Thursday. But if I wanted to play on Saturday I had to practice on Thursday.
>
> As an athlete you want to play, so you tell them what they want to hear. 'I'm fine, and I want to play.' I think that's pretty normal for most athletes. But nowadays the protocol is a little bit different."

Asked if he or any of his teammates had any concussions while in the NFL:

> "There were multiples guys I know who've had multiple ones. By the time my buddy, Zach Miller, was 29 years old he was five or six diagnosed concussions deep. There are a lot of guys like that.
>
> Other than that one time in college where I knew I had a concussion, there wasn't a diagnosed concussion in my NFL career. But there were more times than I can account for when you hit somebody, and your eyes go dizzy and you see little things floating around.
>
> A lot of times you have a constant headache in training camp. You go back to the sidelines a lot of times after running down on kickoff.

You're joking around and telling your buddies you got your bell rung and 'I'm dizzy and I'm seeing stars.' But you're not telling the trainers; you're just trying to stay in the game.

It's kind of a gladiator feeling when you're out there and you want to play. It's not comical, it's not funny. But at the same time you're on the sidelines going, 'Man, I got jacked up on that one.' And the other guy is like, 'Yeah, me too.' That stuff goes on all the time.'

Special teams in the NFL was really what I did most. It's not a glorified job running down there. A lot of my buddies would run down there and separate their shoulder and get it popped back in, then get shot up with some pain medication at halftime and they're back in playing! That's kind of a side of the NFL I think most people never get to see.

I think half the people would probably say they care (I say that because I've been to games in the stands now). To the other half of the people we're gladiators out there. They want to see the big hits.

They don't want to see the refs protecting the defense's receiver; they don't want to see the refs protecting the quarterback. They want to see NFL-type big boy game stuff, so that's kind of what's scary."

When I asked John what the NFL's protocol for treatment and recovery, and regaining playing time was back then:

"I don't really know. I just remember being hurt. The last place you wanted to be was the training room, so you hit it. You didn't want to tell them, because you knew that if you Were out and somebody else went in – and they'd show any glimpse of being just as good or better than you – then you were out and you were done.

> There's a saying: 'You can't make the club in the tub.' In training camp we lived by that because you couldn't be hurt. The only reason I made the team my first year was because when a couple tight ends went down they had no choice but to insert me in there. And when I showed I could play just as well as those guys who were five, six-year veterans, they cut them because they were going to pay me less to do what I proved I could do just as good as them.
>
> As far as protocol goes, I don't really know. I just know that we tried to hide it from them and get better on our own. If we could tolerate the pain and go out there and do it, we were going to do it.
>
> Guys were lining up to shoot up with Toradol before games. 'What's that?' 'Toradol.' 'What does it do?' 'I don't know, but it makes me feel good.' 'Okay. I want some,' was normal. I think before I was there it was even worse as they'd hand out painkillers on the plane ride home and stuff like that.
>
> When Roger Goodell took over as the NFL commissioner in 2006, they started cracking down on some of that stuff. But from just my couple of years there I still saw a lot of cover up (shoot them up with cortisone and Toradol and stuff like that) just to get them out there to play."

John mentioned two blogs he placed on his website relating to tackle football:

> "One was by a parent of a high level kid who played at USC. Another one was by a player who played as a special teams guy in the NFL who took punishment too. It's just one of those topics where I won't truly know how I feel until I have a son. I guess an ultimate test of what my answer is going to be is when my son asks to play tackle football.

As I sit right now, I know how dangerous football can be. But there are many good things it taught me as well (i.e., being part of a team, the discipline, camaraderie and the fearlessness). So there's a lot of great things football can teach young kids.

When I'm coaching these little kids in the weight room I think it's really important to worry about athleticism at a young age. And make sure that they have good footwork and good body mechanics because you can work on all that stuff without getting tackled.

You can play flag football and learn the right footwork, and learn how to play the game.

At some point you're going to have to put the pads on and learn how to play tackle football. I don't know if it's an age thing or just a development thing. But I do know that it's really important to get with coaches who understand what they're doing.

Some kids are afraid, so what do they do when they're afraid? They tuck their head. Luckily I don't remember any real bad injuries. It's a fine line. The kid's got to be ready. They've got to be developed and have some of the fundamentals down before you put the pads on them.

The other part that's hard is some kids develop at a faster age, so you have a strong, fast, explosive kid against a kid who hasn't grown yet. They're the same age so they've got to play on the same league. Some kids have no chance against some of the more developed kids, so I think that's kind of where the danger comes in.

Even in high school there's a difference in kids. A sophomore playing against a fully developed full-grown senior is trouble. At least in the NFL (although there are some freaks out there) we're all fully grown men.

> But I think there's a great disadvantage to some of the kids growing up because they're not as developed as some of the bigger, stronger, faster kids. And there's nothing they can do about it until they grow and their body's ready."

Today there's a push, more so back East than out West, to have kids play flag football until they reach the high school level. I assume it's because when they reach high school football they'll have much more informed, better coaches who know how to teach proper tackling.

There are approximately five million kids from high school down to Little League who play football, and about three million of those are in the Little League program. If you do the math, that's about 600,000 coaches to take care of all those kids. So I think their idea is to play flag football first so they can learn proper footwork, then have them start tackling in high school. For instance, because Tom Brady, Sr. subscribed to that philosophy Tom Brady, Jr. didn't play tackle football until he reached high school (mentioned earlier in Chapter 2):

> "From what I see in the weight room, and the amount of kids I see who fall into that age category, I think I would support that because there are a lot of important things that are missing rather than just a tackling component. If kids have aspirations to go on and play college ball, I think they could miss out on the tackle portion of Little League where they work on becoming more athletic and working on the fundamentals.
>
> Again, sometimes kids are scared against the bigger, stronger and faster kids. They're at a disadvantage because it's not an age thing; it's a when their body's ready thing.
>
> From my experience, I know for a fact that those years are way more crucial for somebody wanting to play in the NFL. You don't really hear of kids not playing in high school and then playing in the NFL. Though I did it without it, I'm not saying it was an easy road.

> But I think if kids didn't tackle it really wouldn't damage their chances of getting that Division I scholarship if they were to only tackle in 9th, 10th, 11th and 12th grades.
>
> I think it forces kids to work on the fundamentals and their athleticism, then worry about hitting when their body is a little bit more ready. So I think I would be for that. The comeback is I learned a lot about toughness, fear and overcoming those obstacles, and becoming a tougher kid through tackle football.
>
> I think it's kind of a gray area topic. Like I said, I won't know until it's my own kid. But if I were to choose right now I think I'd be more on the side of Tom Brady's dad and play flag until high school."

I first met John years ago when he began training my son. Not only was I was extremely impressed with his knowledge of physical training, but how well the kids responded to him. He's trained many of the young men I coached in football and basketball, and when I talk to them about him they all say they had great experiences with him.

Great thanks to John for providing a rare insight into his thoughts as a student and professional athlete. I highly recommend anyone wanting to improve their lives through physical strength and conditioning to work with him at the John Madsen Performance Gym (I included his contact information in the References section at the back of this book).

CHAPTER TWELVE

PROPER TACKLING TECHNIQUES

(Note: All high school photos in this chapter are credited to and courtesy of Dave Sanderson at www.dsandersonpics.com)

While proper tackling won't guarantee the prevention of injuries, it can substantially reduce the risk. If as a parent you're going to allow your child to play tackle football, you have the responsibility to make sure they're tackling properly.

I'm going to share different philosophies when it comes to teaching proper tackling techniques (though I encourage you to do your own research to determine which ones you're most confident with).

Some terms you may have heard on the field to teach techniques are: Bite the ball, break down or buzz, rip, heads-up, face mask to the numbers, wrap and drive.

USA's Heads up Football Techniques

USA breaks their supported tackling technique into five actions (listed below as items 2 through 6). I added number one to their list:

1. Approach
2. Breakdown
3. Buzzing (while gaining ground)
4. Hit Position
5. Shoot
6. Rip

Break Down / Buzzing

The first motion while on approach to prepare for a proper tackle is to break down, which refers to lowering your hips with your body at a 45 degree angle.

Approach

The approach is the initial step in preparing for an effective tackle.

Tracking or approaching the near hip places the player in a proper approach regardless of where they are on the field with respect to the ball carrier.

Breakdown 1 / Buzzing

Breakdown 2 / Buzzing

Breakdown 3 / Buzzing
(Notice how square the tackler's shoulders are to the ball carrier)

Hit Position...

Breakdown 4 / Buzzing -- Hit Position

You'll notice the low hips on the break down. But what you won't see is the next step, which is buzzing or pounding your feet. The key to this step is to keep your feet buzzing, and to always gain ground in a direction toward the ball carrier. Once you stop, your feet you are no longer in an athletic posture to maintain position on the ball carrier. You don't want to stop moving, so you maintain movement toward the ball carrier.

The "bite the ball" philosophy would have the tackler place his face mask on the ball which also places his head in the middle of the impact zone. For that reason, Heads up Football doesn't support the "bite the ball" philosophy.

In this next photo you'll notice the tackler lowers his head and places his shoulder pad in the thigh of the ball carrier. You'll also notice that the tacklers' pads are lower than the ball carrier (reference to the saying "the lowest one wins").

Shoot and Rip

Shoot (Open Hips)

Rip 1

Rip 2

Going back to the approach and breakdown, in the previous photos you can see the tackler squaring his shoulders to the ball carrier, whereas the photos below illustrate a tackler failing to square his shoulders.

If the ball carrier doesn't lose his footing, he could avoid the tackle. (Looking beyond the players in these photos, you'll notice the safety doesn't have any backside help.

If number 20 keeps his footing, he'll take the ball to the house.)

In this position the tackler continues moving to the ball carrier's left.

However, you'll see that when the ball carrier cuts to the right, the tackler is unable to move in that direction.

Because the tackler failed to square his shoulders to the ball carrier, at this point the tackler would have to stop and reverse direction before he could change his motion to follow the ball carrier's cut to the right.

As an example, when you're in your car and you have to slam on the brakes your head and body are forced forward. Since the tackler's head is down, the only thing he can do is stretch his arm out to attempt to tackle the ball carrier, hoping this will cause the carrier to lose his footing and fall. Otherwise, he could avoid the tackle. However, squaring his shoulders and buzzing his feet allows the tackler to move in any direction in reaction to the ball carrier.

This next photo is an example of what I would call "bite the ball." (You can see why USA Football's Heads Up program doesn't like this technique as it puts the tackler's head in the middle of the impact. The technique they teach is to bring the head up prior to impact into the chest, allowing the shoulder pads to become the center of the tackle and absorb the impact.)

Seattle Seahawks' Tackling Techniques

(Photos and the information contained in this section can be found on the Seattle Seahawks' website; the URL is included in the Reference section at the end of the book.)

I fully support the tackling techniques the Seattle Seahawks developed. They finished the 2014-2015 season as the number one overall defense -- as well as the number one passing defense and the number three rushing defense – in spite of losing a very close, tough, well-fought Super Bowl game to the New England Patriots.

The Seahawks break their tackling scheme into six parts:

1. Hawk Tackling
2. Hawk Roll Tackling
3. Profile Tackle
4. Strike Zone
5. Tracking
6. Compression Tackle

According to their head coach, Pete Carroll, inspired by the game of rugby this is a shoulder tackle technique that takes the head out of the tackle. You may be aware that rugby is played without pads or helmets, so this shoulder technique allows the Seahawks to maintain the physicality and integrity of the game while protecting their players.

Hawk Tackling Coaching Points

1. Eyes Through the Thighs
2. Wrap-and-Squeeze
3. Drive for Five

Since Hawk Tackling is a shoulder tackling technique, the focus is on eyes through the thighs, wrap-and-squeeze, and drive for five when necessary.

In the photo below, you can see that number 25 is executing a textbook tackle based on Hawk Tackling. Eyes through the thighs results in the shoulder pads taking most, if not all, of the impact, essentially removing the head from the tackle.

SEA 6 9:22
ATL 0 2ND
2ND & 14
FOX
ND & 14

54
28

This next photo illustrates the wrap-and-squeeze technique. (You'll notice they practice their tackling technique in shorts and without helmets, which looks a lot like the rugby photo below.)

Hawk Roll Tackling Coaching Points

1. Eyes Through the Thighs
2. Wrap-and-Squeeze
3. Roll

Hawk Roll Tackling is the same technique as the Hawk Tackling mentioned above, with the addition of the roll. The picture below is an example of the roll added to the Hawk Tackle.

Hawk Roll Tackling is practiced at full speed using pads

Profile Tackle Coaching Points

1. Attack the Closest Pec
2. Wrap
3. Drive for five

The Profile Tackle is a chest-high tackle that attacks the closest chest pec muscle of the ball carrier.

Notice the player's head placement. The ball carrier in the Hawk Tackle most often goes down immediately.

Drive for Five (steps)

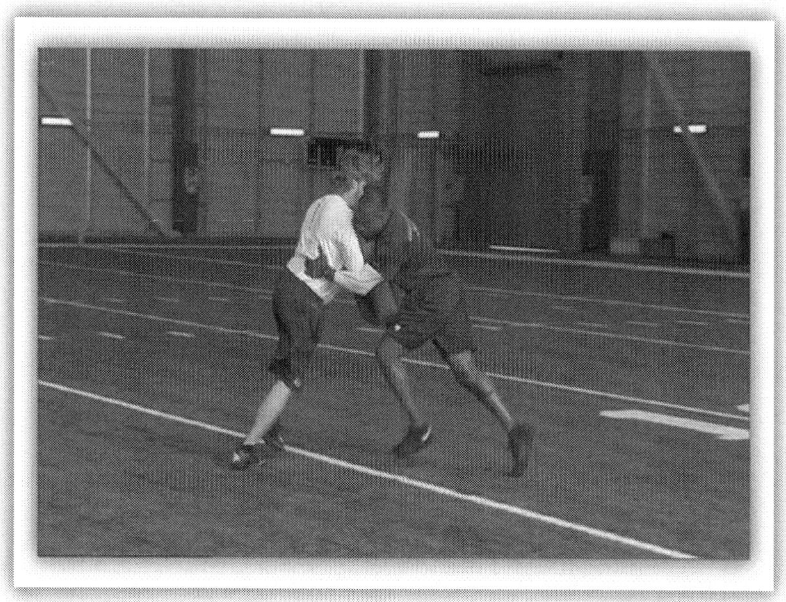

Strike Zone

The Strike Zone refers to tackling a defenseless player. The zone is below the neck and above the knees, much like a strike zone in baseball. Contact is always with the shoulder. This technique removes the head of both the ball carrier and the tackler from the play.

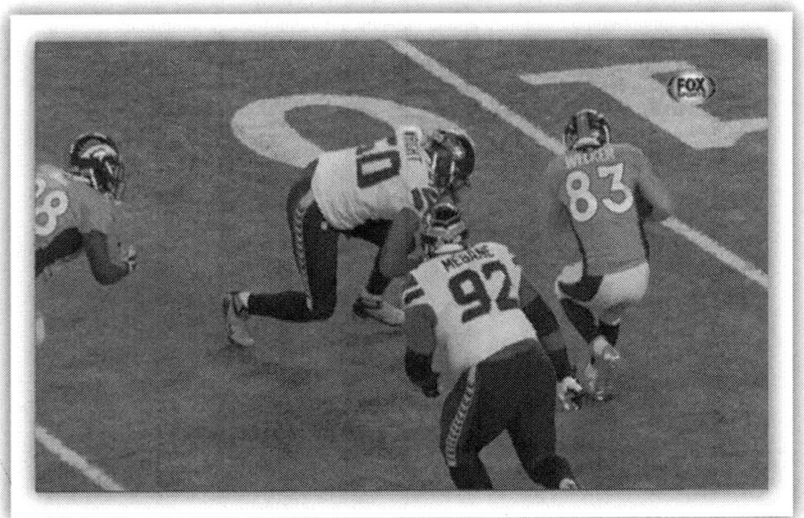

Even though this play was originally flagged for an illegal hit, the League later reclassified it as a legal hit. Notice that even with an extremely powerful impact, the heads of the ball carrier and tackler are out of the impact zone.

NFL CBS

NFL CBS
DET 31
CLE 17
DET R. BUSH: 17 RUSH, 78 YDS
FINAL

Compression Tackling

Compression Tackling is applying the Hawk Tackling technique to two or more tacklers. Both follow the coaching points by attacking the near hip.

Notice the approach attacking near hip of ball carrier

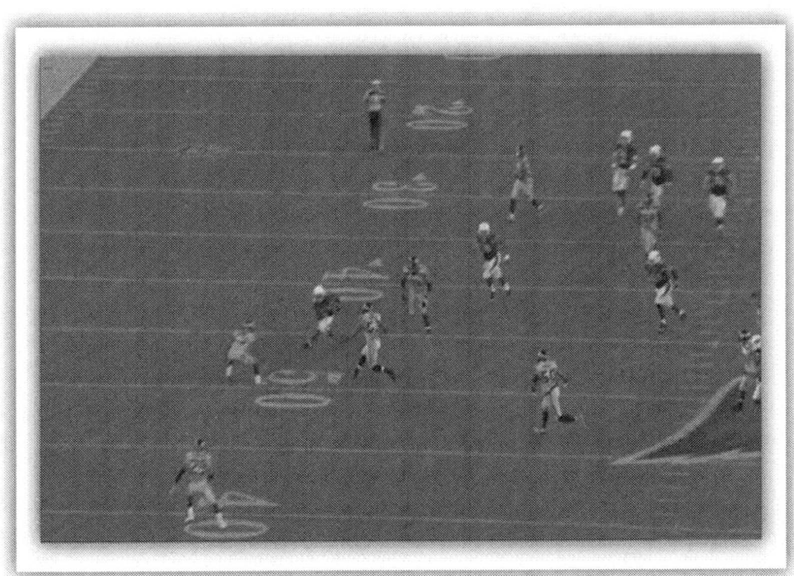

Notice the Hawk Tackle on the right hip of the ball carrier, and the Profile Tackle on the left hip of the ball carrier

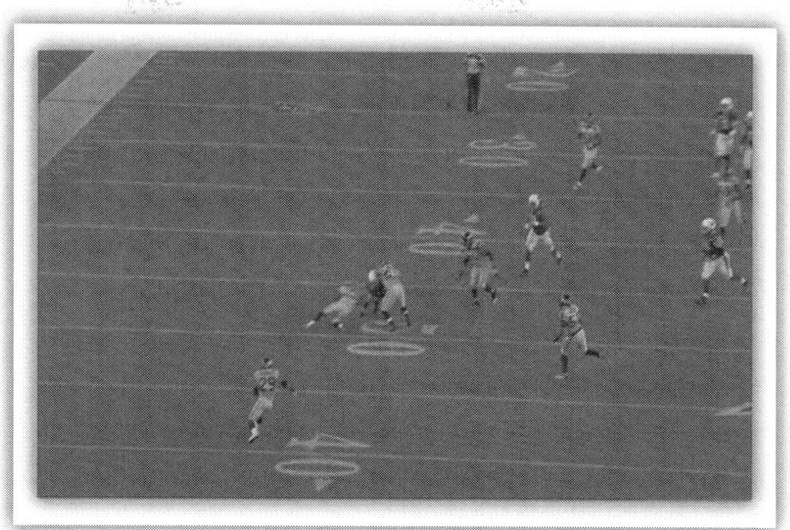

Tracking

Tracking is closing the distance with the ball carrier while maintaining leverage. The target is the near hip of the ball carrier.

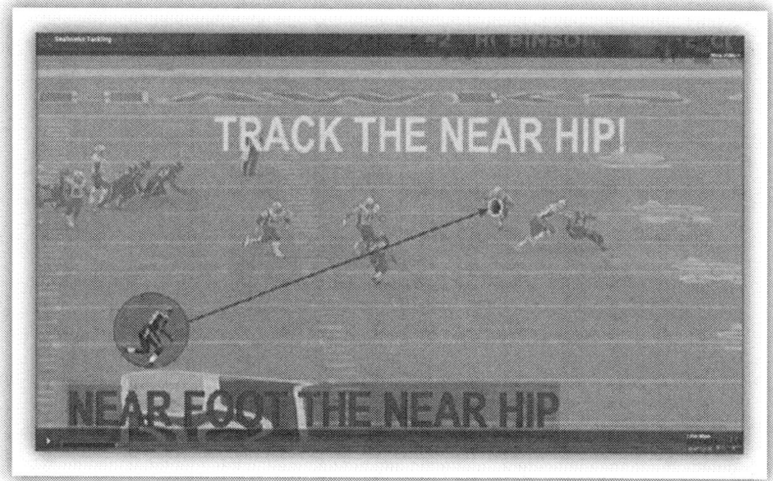

You'll find many different philosophies and techniques for teaching proper tackling. I like the fact that the Hawk Tackling technique removes the heads of the ball carrier and the tackler from the impact zone.

Obviously I'm not able to adequately present all of the information in this book, so I recommend that you spend some time on the Seattle Seahawks' website, and watch the video they produced to teach their techniques.

The bottom line is that you as a parent must take responsibility for the safety of your children who are playing tackle football. Education and implementation of the education is the key to safer football practices.

CHAPTER THIRTEEN

PROPER FITTING OF SHOULDER PADS AND HELMETS

Proper Fitting of Shoulder Pads

Step 1

Using a flexible measuring tape, measure around the biggest part of the child's chest and just under their armpits. This task is somewhat difficult to do, so the child should have a parent or friend do the measuring for them.

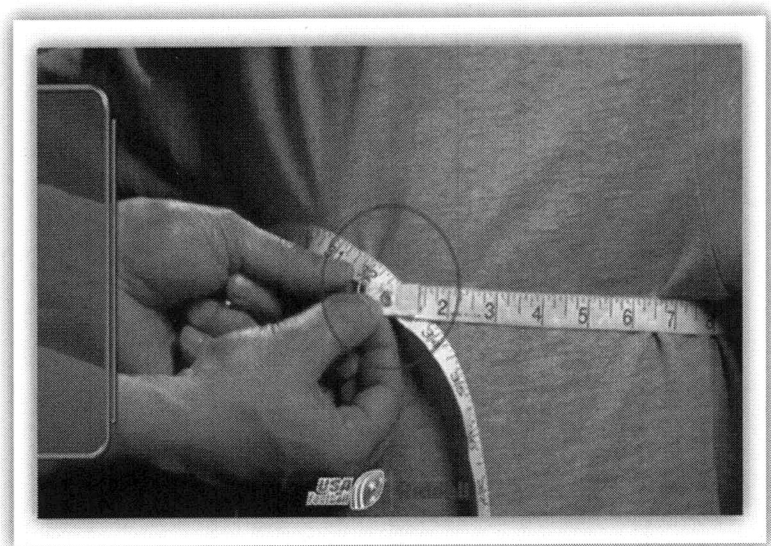

Step 2

Measure their shoulders all the way across, including the tops of the Humerus (the long bone in the arm or forelimb that runs from the shoulder to the elbow).

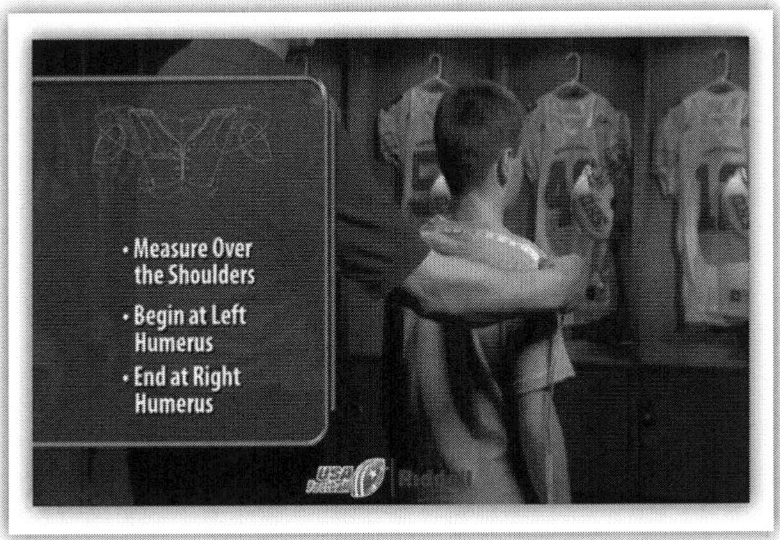

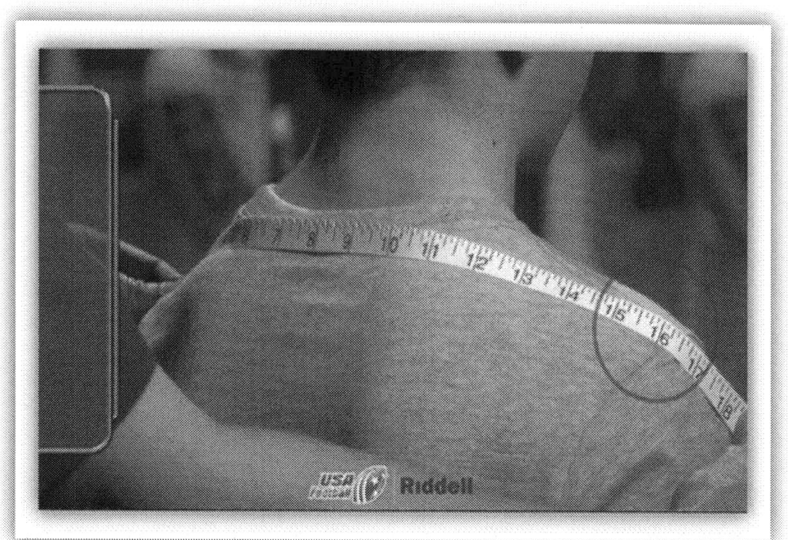

Step 4

When determining proper shoulder pad size, use the chart that comes with the make and model of the shoulder pad as every manufacturer sizes pads differently.

Below is an example of the sizing chart for the Riddell Youth Phenom Shoulder Pad.

Riddell

YOUTH PHENOM SHOULDER PAD SIZE CHART

PAD SIZE	SHOULDER WIDTH	CHEST CIRCUMFERENCE
XS	10"-11"	24"-26"
S	11"-12"	26"-28"
M	12"-13"	28"-30"
L	13"-14"	30"-32"
XL	14"-15"	32"-34"
XXL	15"-16"	34"-36"

This is only a guide. Player's measurements, shoulder pad sizes and actual fit may vary.
*For youth shoulder pads, the shoulder width measurement has more of a direct correlation to proper fit.

Step 5

Put on the shoulder pad to confirm proper fitting. It should fit comfortably without any pinching or binding. The child should be able to rotate their head without their neck moving the pad.

Make sure their shoulder blades are covered, and the Humerus on both sides of their shoulders is also covered.

• No Pinching
or Binding
• 1/4" Above Humerus
• Sternum, Scapula
& Rhomboid
USA Football
Riddell

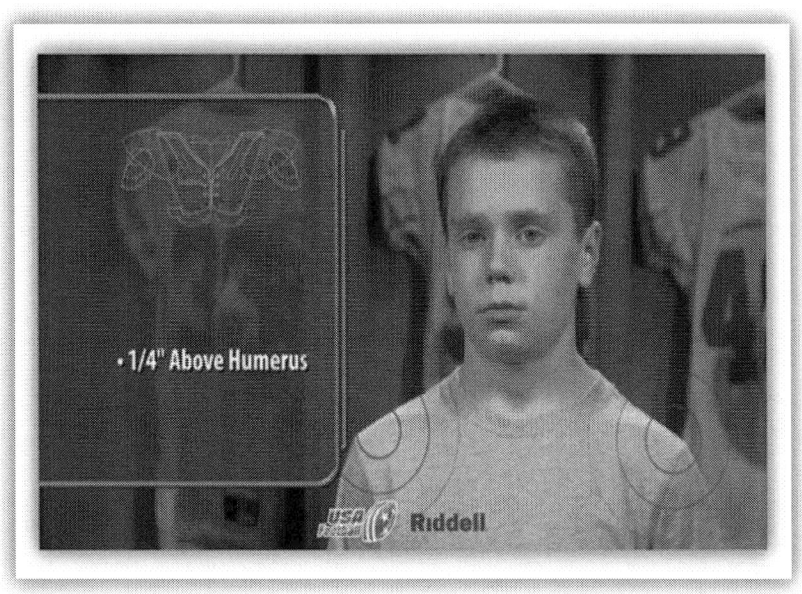
• 1/4" Above Humerus
USA Football
Riddell

Step 6

A properly fitted shoulder pad should allow the child to move in all football movements with little resistance (i.e., lifting their arms to catch a football, tucking the ball high and tight, and proper arm and shoulder movement while running).

Have them stretch their arms out to the sides, then in front of them. Have them move around briskly to make sure the shoulder pads are snug, but not tight enough to restrict their breathing or any of their torso movements.

Then have them raise their arms straight up to make sure the neck rolls don't touch their skin. When the top of the shoulder pads are sharply tapped, they shouldn't feel any pain or discomfort.

Proper Fitting of Helmets

The proper fitting of the helmet is crucial in preventing injury including concussions. It's a simple but very important process in protecting the player.

The helmet should not move independent of the head. If the child is able to shift the helmet without moving their head, the helmet isn't fit properly. A loose helmet won't absorb the impact as well as it should.

Each manufacturer's fitting instructions are specific to the helmets they produce. In fact, each helmet within a single manufacturer will most likely have its own fitting instructions.

Step 1

Measure the diameter of the player's head one inch (1") above the eyebrow.

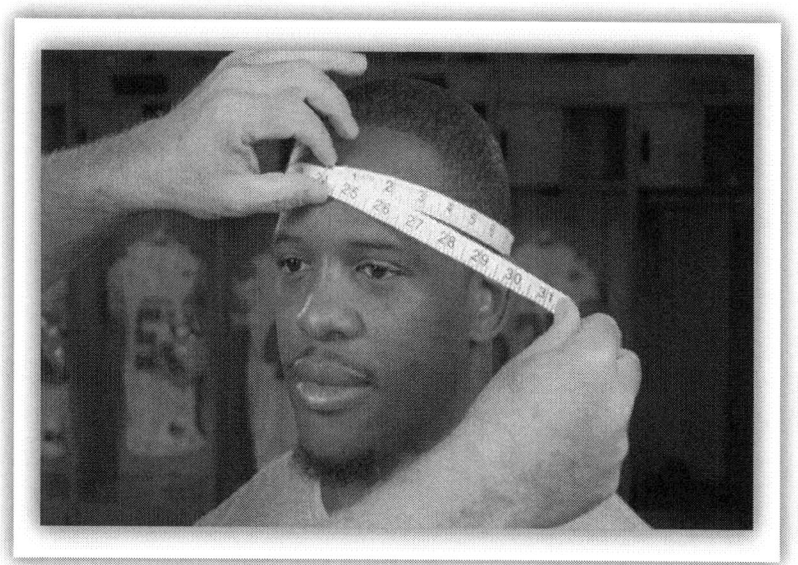

Step 2

Once again, it's critical to use the manufacture's chart that matches the helmet the player will be wearing. Although many manufacturers use similar sizing, there may be substantial differences.

It's also important to understand the sizing chart gives you an basic idea on what helmet size will fit the player properly, but without measuring their head you can't be assured of a 100% correct fit.

Therefore, don't simply read the chart and give the player the size helmet it suggests as it can be wrong. Take the time to be assured the helmet they're getting is the right one for the shape and size of their head as everyone is different.

Schutt Youth Helmet Sizing Chart		
Size	Head Size	Head Circumference
XXS	6 - 6 1/4	19" - 19 1/2"
XS	6 3/8 - 6 1/2	20" - 20 1/2"
S	6 5/8 - 6 3/4	20 3/4" - 21 1/4"
M	6 7/8 - 7	21 1/2" - 22"
L	7 1/8 - 7 1/4	22 1/4" - 22 3/4"
XL	7 3/8 - 7 1/2	23" - 23 1/2"

Step 3

When putting on the helmet to ensure a proper fit, gently pull the sides out to allow the player's head to easily slide inside.

When confirming proper fitting with the jaw pads, make sure they're snug without pushing in on the cheeks. The pad should also be flush with the jaw.

Below is the full fitting instructions for Riddell's 360 series helmet:

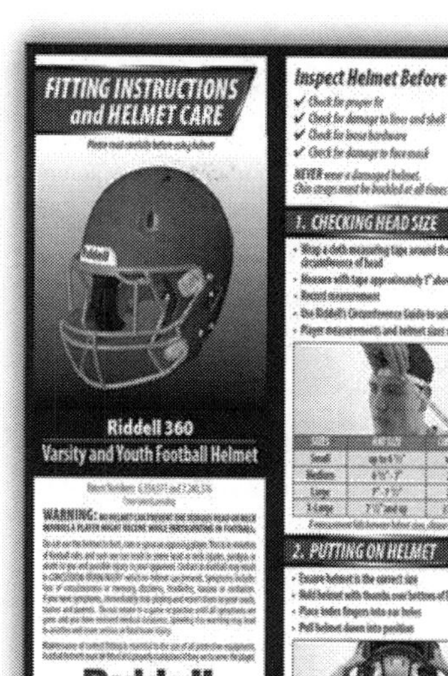

Inspect Helmet Before Each Use
✔ Check for proper fit
✔ Check for damage to liner and shell
✔ Check for loose hardware
✔ Check for damage to face mask
NEVER wear a damaged helmet.
Chin straps must be buckled at all times during play.

1. CHECKING HEAD SIZE

2. PUTTING ON HELMET

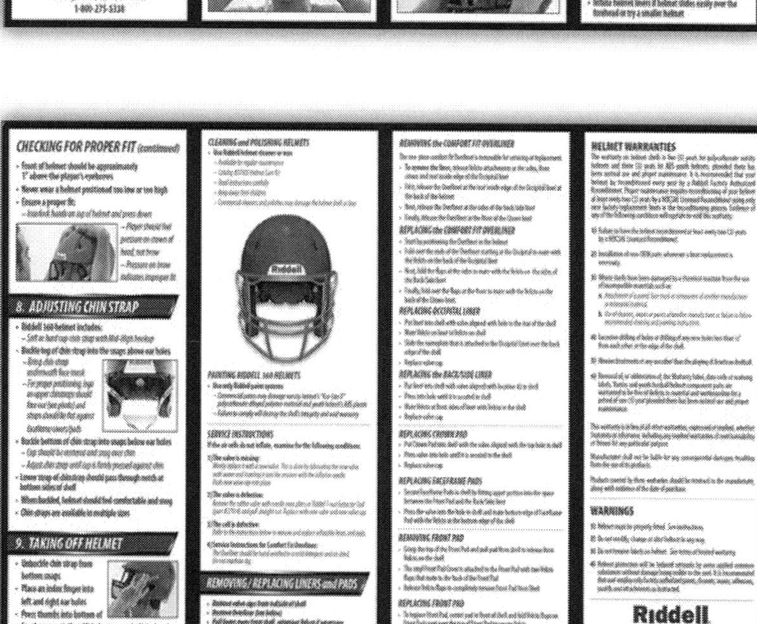

Conclusion

SHOULD OR SHOULDN'T YOUTH PLAY TACKLE FOOTBALL?

I wish to emphasize the fact that tackle football can be, and often is, a very dangerous sport. The time when we as parents dropped our kids off at practice, then showed up for the games and called that support, are over.

Even though I've provided information on safer tackling techniques, it would be impossible for me to cover every philosophy or training available on tackle football. There isn't one technique that's perfect for every player, nor is there a technique or combination of techniques that can prevent all injuries.

If you're going to allow your children to play tackle football, it's YOUR responsibility to invest the time and attention to learn, teach and implement the techniques you're most confident in. My hope is that as you work with your child you'll find the same passion in coaching I have, and that your passion will create a positive influence in the lives of many others.

Confessional from the Author

While attending a coaching clinic in Nevada, I heard the keynote speaker (the head coach for a local college team) say, "Yes, tackle football is safe." I thought about the controversies surrounding the issues of safety in football, and decided right there and to write a book about that very subject matter.

While conducting my research -- and due to my subsequent experiences in tackle football as a coach -- I learned a great deal about concussions as well as other injuries.

So my confession is I'm no longer convinced that tackle football is safe for the youth of America.

As previously mentioned, my two older sons have played football, and I have an eight-year-old son who will be old enough to begin tackle football. Watching my children play sports gives me great enjoyment, so I was excited about being able to watch him play as well.

However, knowing what I know now about the ramifications of potential injuries – and after reading Mark Hyman's book, *Concussions and Our Kids: America's Leading Expert on How to Protect Young Athletes and Keep Sports Safe*_-- my decision to allow my youngest son to play tackle football has come into question.

My eldest son was flipped upside down while playing basketball. Now as I look back I believe he received an impact concussion when his head hit the floor. So I'm considering not allowing my youngest son to play until he's fourteen when his body is stronger.

I guess that puts me in the situation many of you are in, which is to make the right choice about allowing your kids to play potentially harmful sports.

Chris Borland, Linebacker, Retires at 24, Citing Health Concerns from a Career in the NFL

In 2015, Chris Borland of the San Francisco 49ers retired from football at the young age of 24, citing a concern over the potential long-term health risks that could result from a long career in football, especially as it relates to concussions.

He suffered an apparent concussion during the 2014-2015 spring training that led him to a season of study and education on the potential health issues resulting from concussions. After consulting with doctors and former NFL player David Meggyesy, Borland said it wasn't a difficult decision to make:

> "I mean, it could potentially kill you. I know that's a drastic way to put it, but it is a possibility that really puts it in perspective to me. To me, it just wasn't what I wanted to do."

Borland was under a four-year contract with the 49ers, and was worth just under $3 million. He made just over $1 million playing in the NFL, but may be required to return more than $400,000 of his signing bonus:

> "I can relate from the outside looking in that it wouldn't make sense to a lot of people. I've had close friends who have said, 'Well, why don't you just play one more year? It's a lot more money, and you probably won't get hurt.' I just don't want to get in a situation where I'm negotiating my health for money. Who knows how many hits is too many?"

When Chris informed former St. Louis Cardinal David Meggyesy that he would probably retire, Meggyesy supported him and offered some advice:

> "I just told him that depending on how you do it, you could do a lot of good by getting people, especially parents of young kids, to get them to think about, *should I let my kid play football?*"

In an interview with *Outside the Lines*, Borland made it clear that he wasn't "eager to wave the banner, or be a poster child for anything." When questioned about that very profound statement he responded, "My health is more important than a career in football."

Borland also received the full support of his father who stated he was "relieved."

Following the announcement by Borland, and during an interview with *NFL Total Access*, Dr. Joseph Maroon made comments that sparked a great deal of controversy. In reference to Chronic Traumatic Encephalopathy (CTE) he stated:

> "I think the problem of CTE, although real, is it's being over-exaggerated, and it's being extrapolated to youth football and to high school football."

Dr. Maroon (the Pittsburgh Steelers' team neurosurgeon; and the board-certified clinical professor of Neurological Surgery at the University of Pittsburgh Medical Center) went on to state that...

> "There are…more injuries to kids falling off bikes, scooters, falling in playgrounds than there are in youth football. I think again, it's never been safer. Can we improve? Yes. We have to do better all the time to make it safer."

Referencing the improved tackling techniques, as well as the recent rule changes and improvements to recognizing, treating and clearing players by the medical staff, Dr. Maroon believes the sport has never been safer.

Assessing Their Level of Fear

I concur with Dr. Maroon's statement that Chris Borland made the correct decision for him to retire from football:

> "When an athlete is fearful of any injury, it's time to get out. You can't play with apprehension in any sport and be as good as you can be."

I would add that to play with fear or apprehension drastically increases the possibility of an injury including concussions. Which leads to one of the most important assessments you have to make as a parent regarding your kids and football. Will they or are they playing scared?

If you make that assessment in the affirmative, I recommend you give your child one to three more years before you allow them to play (of course, assessing at that time if they've overcome their fear. If they haven't, the sport may not be for them at all.)

If there's any doubt your child will enjoy playing football without fear, I recommend that you sign them up for flag football for a year or more which will allow them to play the sport without the physicality of tackling.

There's absolutely nothing wrong with your child playing flag football; in fact, one of our standout players at Riverton High had originally played flag football as a youngster.

There's also nothing wrong with not allowing your child to play football as it isn't for everyone, especially if they've expressed the desire not to play (meaning, it should be up to them whether or not it's a sport they want to play).

I have to admit there have been times when I forced my kids to play a sport they didn't want to play. However, over the years I learned to recognize the difference between a child who doesn't want to play due to laziness, or if they truly don't want to play.

Simply put, there are times when youth don't know what's best for them. So I believe an 8, 10 or even a 15-year-old should NOT be allowed to make their own decision on such matters without consultation and approval from their parents.

So how do you know when the time is right for your child to play a sport, including tackle football? Unlike many other sports, a player can play tackle football later in life and still make a good impact for their team.

Therefore, there's nothing wrong with the decision to hold your child out of the sport until they're physically, mentally, and emotionally ready to play without fear or apprehension.

There's an appropriate growing concern surrounding tackle football at all levels. The many reports on the tragedies, and long-term health challenges (including death and suicides) in the NFL with Chronic Traumatic Encephalopathy (CTE) has caused many parents to question if football is safe enough for their kids.

I can't tell you what decision you should make when faced with the important decision of allowing your child to play. That decision must be yours, but now at least you have the information to make a well-informed decision.

The bottom line is parents shouldn't sign their kids up for a sport or events without first doing their due diligence to determine the safety and risks involved. As parents, the responsibility is ours to make those kinds of determinations due to the potential risks involved.

As of this writing, my wife Tish and I made the decision not to allow our eight-year old son to play tackle football. This may change after a year or two of flag football, but for now he's not playing tackle football.

I've presented you with both sides of the argument, and the pros and cons of playing tackle football. Since the safety of our children is among the most important responsibility that we as parents have, we need to trust our instincts to guide us to a correct decision.

God bless you and your family's safety and well-being.

Alan Jackson

MOTIVATIONAL QUOTES

NOTE: This list is from "Inspirational Quotes for Sports Coaches compiled by Bo Hanson. The URL for his book on Amazon.com is in References.

'Success is peace of mind which is a direct result of self-satisfaction in knowing you did your best to become the best you are capable of becoming." ~**John Wooden, Basketball**

"The interesting thing about coaching is that you have to trouble the comfortable, and comfort the troubled." ~**Ric Charlesworth, Hockey**

"Winning is not a sometime thing; it's an all-time thing. You don't win once in a while, you don't do things right once in a while, you do them right all the time. Winning is habit. Unfortunately, so is losing." ~**Vince Lombardi, American Football**

"Most people get excited about games, but I've got to be excited about practice, because that's my classroom." ~**Pat Summitt, Basketball**

"Leadership is more about responsibility than ability!" ~ **Jim Tunney, American Football**

"To be as good as it can be, a team has to buy into what you as the coach are doing. They have to feel you're a part of them and they're a part of you." ~**Bobby Knight**

"You don't demand respect, you earn it." ~**Steve Seidler**

"The only place that success comes before work is in the dictionary." ~**Vince Lombardi, American Football**

"It's what you learn, after you know it all, that counts." **~John Wooden, Basketball**

"Never quit. It is the easiest cop-out in the world. Set a goal and don't quit until you attain it. When you do attain it, set another goal, and don't quit until you reach it. Never quit." **~ Bear Bryant, American Football**

"Coaches have to watch for what they don't want to see and listen to what they don't want to hear." **~John Madden, American Football**

"Attitudes are contagious. Are yours worth catching?" **~Anonymous**

"Victory or defeat is not determined at the moment of crisis, but rather in the long and unspectacular period of preparation." **~Anonymous**

"The [best] coaches... know that the job is to win... know that they must be decisive, that they must phase people through their organizations, and at the same time they are sensitive to the feelings, loyalties, and emotions that people have toward one another. If you don't have these feelings, I do not know how you can lead anyone. I have spent many sleepless nights trying to figure out how I was going to phase out certain players for whom I had strong feelings, but that was my job. I wasn't hired to do anything but win." **~Bill Walsh, American Football**

"Things turn out best for those who make the best of the way things turn out." **~John Wooden, Basketball**

"A coach should never be afraid to ask questions of anyone he could learn from." **~Bobby Knight, Basketball**

"A common mistake among those who work in sport is spending a disproportional amount of time on "x's and o's" as compared to time spent learning about people." **~Mike Krzyzewski, Basketball**

"Let me tell you what winning means.... you're willing to go longer, work harder, give more than anyone else." **~Vince Lombardi, American Football**

"All coaching is, is taking a player where he can't take himself." **~Bill McCartney, American Football**

"I found out that if you are going to win games, you had better be ready to adapt." **~Scotty Bowman, Hockey**

"I want my team to be more detached from the wins and losses and be more focused on doing the little things well. When you focus on getting the win, it can suffocate you, especially during the playoffs when the pressure gets thick." **~Sue Enquist, Softball**

"An acre of performance is worth a whole world of promise." **~Red Auerbach, Basketball**

"I think the most important thing about coaching is that you have to have a sense of confidence about what you're doing. You have to be a salesman and you have to get your players, particularly your leaders, to believe in what you're trying to accomplish on the basketball floor." **~Phil Jackson, Basketball**

"A winner never whines." **~Paul Brown, American Football**

"Be more concerned with your character than your reputation. Because your character is what you really are, while your reputation is merely what others think you are." **~John Wooden, Basketball**

"First master the fundamentals." **~Larry Bird, Basketball**
"Good teams become great ones when the members trust each other enough to surrender the 'me' for the 'we'." **~Phil Jackson, Basketball**

"Practice doesn't make perfect. Perfect practice makes perfect." **~Vince Lombardi, American Football**

"I'd say handling people is the most important thing you can do as a coach. I've found every time I've gotten into trouble with a player, it's because I wasn't talking to him enough." **~Lou Holtz, American Football**

"Nothing great was ever achieved without enthusiasm." **~Bobby Knight - Henry David Thoreau**

"Champions keep playing until they get it right." **~Billie Jean King, Tennis**

"There is another side [to ego] that can wreck a team or an organization. That is being distracted by your own importance. It can come from your insecurity in working with others. It can be the need to draw attention to yourself in the public arena. It can be a feeling that others are a threat to your own territory. These are all negative manifestations of ego, and if you are not alert to them, you get diverted and your work becomes diffused. Ego in these cases makes people insensitive to how they work with others and it ends up interfering with the real goal of any group efforts." **~Bill Walsh, American Football**

"If we were supposed to talk more than we listen we would have two mouths and one ear." **~Mark Twain**

"Nothing will work unless you do." **~John Wooden, Basketball**

"You can motivate by fear, and you can motivate by reward. But both those methods are only temporary. The only lasting thing is self-motivation." **~Homer Rice, Football**

"Good coaching may be defined as the development of character, personality and habits of players, plus the teaching of fundamentals and team play." **~Claire Bee, Basketball**

"The absolute bottom line in coaching is organization and preparing for practice." **~Bill Walsh, American Football**

"When I was a young coach I used to say, 'Treat everybody alike.' That's bull. Treat everybody fairly." **~Bear Bryant, American Football**

"Winning isn't everything, it's the only thing. If you can shrug off a loss, you can never be a winner!" **~Vince Lombardi, American Football**

"The best motivation always comes from within." **~Michael Johnson**

"The definition of courage is going from defeat to defeat with enthusiasm." **~Winston Churchill**

"If you have something critical to sat to a player, preface it by saying something positive. That way when you get to the criticism, at least you know he'll be listening." **~Bud Grant, American Football**

"Two cars parked side by side - one is a supercar, the other an old family sedan. Both have the same potential until someone gets in to the supercar and drives it flat out. The coach can have the best strategy, but unless it's driven its potential means nothing." **~John Schuh**

"People thrive on positive reinforcement. They can take only a certain amount of criticism and you may lose them altogether if you criticize them in a personal way... you can make a point without being personal. Don't insult or belittle your people. Instead of getting more out of them you will get less." **~Bill Walsh, American Football**

"Get the Buy In, Coach the Mind, The Rest then Follows." **~Robin Clarkson**

"The real winners are the people who look at every situation with an expectation that they can make it work or make it better." **~Pletcher**

"I have learned over the years how to hold a team together. How to lift some men up, how to calm others down, until finally they've got one heartbeat, together, a team." **~Bear Bryant, American Football**

"I enjoy winning and very much dislike losing- but I did not allow either of them to obsess me. I was a silent loser, believing that if you won you said little, and if you lost you said even less." **~Paul Brown, American Football**

"The more I have been involved in Football, the more I realize that individual talent is minimized or maximized by the environment those blokes go into." **~ Leigh Matthews, Australian Football League**

"Innovation involves anticipation. It is having a broad base of knowledge on your subject and an ability to see where the end game is headed. Use all your knowledge to get their first. Set the trend and make the competition counter you." **~Bill Walsh, American Football**

"Failure is only the opportunity to begin again more intelligently." **~Henry Ford**

"Make sure that team members know they are working with you, not for you." **~ John Wooden**

"My responsibility is leadership, and the minute I get negative, that is going to have an influence on my team." **~Don Shula**

"If you only ever give 90% in training then you will only ever give 90% when it matters." **~Michael Owen**

"The key is not the will to win. Everybody has that. It is the will to prepare to win that is important." **~Bobby Knight**

"When people ask me now if I miss coaching UCLA basketball games, the national championships, the attention, the trophies, and everything that goes with them, I tell them this: I miss the practices." **~John Wooden**

"Don't ever ask a player to do something he doesn't have the ability to do. He'll just question your ability as a coach, not his as an athlete." **~Lou Holtz**

"Our emphasis is on execution, not winning." **~Pat Summitt**

"The general feeling is, if you don't treat everyone the same you're showing partiality. To me, that's when you show the most partiality, when you treat everyone the same. You must give each individual the treatment that you feel he earns and deserves, recognizing at all times that you're imperfect and you're going to be incorrect oftentimes in your judgment." **~John Wooden**

"I've never felt my job was to win basketball games - rather, that the essence of my job as a coach was to do everything I could to give my players the background necessary to succeed in life." **~Bobby Knight**

"Today I will do what others won't, so tomorrow I can accomplish what others can't."
~Jerry Rice

"There may be people that have more talent than you, but there's no excuse for anyone to work harder than you do."
~Derek Jeter

"Dedication requires determination and determination requires dedication. Being number one means to be both, but being both doesn't make number one." ~ Erin McKinney

"A Champion, is one who will accept a defeat graciously, and a victory with humility." ~Tino

<u>URLs for inspirational speeches in sports:</u>

Inspirational Quotes for Sport Coaches, Compiled by Bo Hanson.
http://www.amazon.com/gp/product/B00H523UP8/ref=as_li_ss_tl?ie=UTF8&camp=1789&creative=390957&creativeASIN=B00H523UP8&linkCode=as2&tag=wwwathleteass-20

"Top 10 Inspirational Speeches in Sports History" (29 January, 2013): White Cover Magazine.

http://www.whitecovermag.com/2013/01/top-10-inspirational-speeches-in-sports-history.html

Waters, Preston (27 September, 2012): "The Most Inspirational Speeches in Sports History."

http://elitedaily.com/sports/inspirational-speeches-sports-history/

REFERENCES

Alic, Steve, Director of Communications (20 May, 2013): *USA Football Releases Preliminary Data in Study Examining Youth Football Player Health and Safety.* http://usafootball.com/health-safety/usa-football-releases-preliminary-date-study-examining-youth-football-player-health-an#sthash.kFXHV6BO.dpuf

CDC Concussion Chart.
www.cdc.gov

Coach John Wooden Quotes.
http://www.inspire21.com/quotes/quotes/JohnWooden

"Concussion in Sports" (re. Steve Young).
http://www.cbsnews.com/pictures/concussions-in-sports/6/

Donaldson, Amy (24 September, 2013: *Taking a Stand: Union High coach suspends entire football team in lesson about character.* Deseret News. http://www.deseretnews.com/article/865587020/Taking-a-stand-Union-High-coach-suspends-entire-football-team-in-lesson-about-character.html?pg=all

Farrey, Tom (22 February, 2012): *Study: Impact of Youth Head Hit Severe.* http://espn.go.com/espn/otl/story/_/id/7601017/study-impact-kids-football-head-hits-severe-college-games

Fitting Instructions and Helmet Care
http://team.riddell.com/wp-content/uploads/360_web.pdf

Football Heat Acclimatization Guidelines.
http://www.uhsaa.org/football/2013/FootballAcclimization%20 Guidelines.pdf ... and http://usafootball.com/health-safety/heat-preparedness

Goldberg, Dr. Alan. *What Makes a Good Coach?* Competitive Advantage: Sports Psychology, Peak Performance and Overcoming Fears & Blocks https://www.competitivedge.com/special-%E2%80%9Cwhat-makes-good-coach%E2%80%9D

Gostkowski, Amy. *What Makes a Great Coach?* USA Hockey Magazine (10/2009 issue). http://webcache.googleusercontent.com/search?q=cache:qho7-gg4pIYJ:www.usahockeymagazine.com/article/2009-10/what-makes-great-coach+&cd=5&hl=en&ct=clnk&gl=us

Hyman, Mark. (6 November, 2012). *Why Kids Under 14 Should Not Play Tackle Football.* http://ideas.time.com/2012/11/06/why-kids-under-14-should-not-play-tackle-football/

Liesik, Geoff (24 September, 2013: Union High School Football Letter. Deseret News. http://www.deseretnews.com/article/865587039/Union-High-School-football-coach-releases-character-letter.html?pg=all

Pamphilon, Sean. *The United States of Football.*
http://theusof.com;
and http://elitedaily.com/sports/inspirational-speeches-sports-history

Reilly, Rick (14 March, 2000) for Sports Illustrated: *Coach John Wooden: A Paragon Rising Above the Madness.* http://www.inspire21.com/stories/sportsstories/coachjohnwooden

Re. Ricardo Portillo:

> *Utah Referee in Coma After Attack* (21 May, 2014): http://msn.foxsports.com/foxsoccer/usa/story/Utah-referee-ricardo-portillo-in-coma-from-teenage-player-attack-remains-in-critical-condition-050213

and...

'I was frustrated at the ref and caused his death': Teenager pleads guilty to killing referee by punching him in the head during soccer game (5 August, 2013): Daily Mail http://www.dailymail.co.uk/news/article-2385028/Ricardo-Portillo-death-Jose-Domingo-Teran-pleads-guilty-killing-Utah-soccer-referee.html#ixzz37ZDX29f2

Today's Helmets
www.Schuttsports.com; www.gamedayr.com

Turley, Kyle
http://en.wikipedia.org/wiki/Kyle_Turley

Utah High School Football Coach Suspends Entire Team to Build Character (25 September, 2013).
http://www.foxnews.com/us/2013/09/25/utah-football-coach-suspends-entire-team-to-build-character/

Virginia Tech, Wake Forest University announce youth football publication and new 'KIDS' head impact study" (24 February, 2012).
http://www.vtnews.vt.edu/articles/2012/02/022412-engineering-youthfootballhelmetstudyresults.html

Photo Credits:

"Crazy Legs" Hirsch (1948 Rams): www.pasttimesports.biz
Knute Rockne (1906): www.pasttimesports.biz
Seattle Seahawks:
"Hawk Tackling" http://www.seahawks.com
and... http://www.seahawks.com/videos photos/videos/Seahawks-Tackling/af5b80dd-7e39-4519-8b80-ad558292b1a
Shoulder Pad and Helmet Fitting: www.sportsunlimitedinc.com, usafootball.com, riddell.com

ABOUT THE AUTHOR

Alan Jackson's greatest passions are his wife Tish, his seven children including a daughter and son-in law, his beautiful granddaughter, and of course sports.

He's coached his kids in baseball, basketball and football, and now enjoys coaching youth football at the high school level in Riverton, Utah.

Alan didn't play many sports when he was growing up, as there weren't the opportunities there are today. But one opportunity became a passion for motocross. Rain, snow, sleet or a hot summer day couldn't keep him off of his dirt bike.

Self-employed since the age of 22, Alan has been able to make the time for his children and their activities.

His eldest daughter played basketball for Riverton High, and was part of the team that placed second in the state tournament. She went on to play a season for the BYU Hawaii basketball team, and also placed second in state in the high jump the year her high school team won the state tournament in track. She's currently preparing to become a firefighter, and resides in Utah with her husband who's an officer in the Army Reserves.

His eldest son played many sports including football and basketball, but his real passion was golf. As of this writing, he's a Marine stationed at Camp Pendleton in Southern California where he resides with his amazing wife and beautiful daughter.

His middle son is a tremendous athlete who played many years of competitive baseball, football, and basketball (his real passion). With several coaches interested in his abilities, he hopes to secure funding for his college education through basketball.

Alan's youngest daughter is just entering high school sports, and he's excited to see her compete at that level. She's a 5'11" 15-year-old who can handle the basketball well enough to play point, but also shoots well enough to play the shooting guard. She's also been known to make a shot from three to four feet outside the three-point line.

His eight-year-old son is just gaining interest in sports (as mentioned earlier, he's not going to play tackle football until they feel he's ready).

With their home base in Utah, the Jacksons have been known to pack up their motorhome and drive straight to New York for a baseball tournament at Cooperstown. One trip consisted of 7,500 miles cross-country for 25 days beginning in New York, ending in North Carolina with everywhere else in between.

OTHER BOOKS BY ALAN JACKSON:

Strategies for Avoiding Foreclosure: A Real Estate Expert's Guide to Keeping Your Home and Preventing Bankruptcy

Amazon Kindle: http://www.amazon.com/Strategies-Avoiding-Foreclosure-Preventing-Bankruptcy/dp/1499394306/ref=sr_1_8?s=books&ie=UTF8&qid=1405456407&sr=1-8&keywords=alan+jackson

CONTACT AND SOCIAL MEDIA INFORMATION:

Youth Tackle Football Facebook Page:
https://www.facebook.com/youthtacklefootball

Personal Facebook Page:
https://www.facebook.com/alan.jackson.338?fref=pb&hc_location=friends_tab

To Contact Alan for speaking engagements, or for further information about this book or his coaching program:
tacklingtacklefootball@gmail.com

Made in the USA
Lexington, KY
09 January 2018